The
HOMESTEAD
SOURDOUGH
Cookbook

GEORGIA VAROZZA

TEN PEAKS PRESS®
EUGENE, OR

Cover photo © Yulia Khlebnikova / Unsplash.com

Cover and interior design by Dugan Design Group

For bulk or special sales, please call 1 (800) 547-8979.

Email: Customerservice@hhpbooks.com

.TEN PEAKS PRESS is a federally registered trademark of The Hawkins Children's LLC. Harvest House Publishers, Inc., is the exclusive licensee of this trademark.

THE HOMESTEAD SOURDOUGH COOKBOOK

Copyright © 2022 by Georgia Varozza

Published by Ten Peaks Press, an imprint of Harvest House Publishers

Eugene, Oregon 97408

ISBN 978-0-7369-8440-9 (pbk.)

ISBN 978-0-7369-8441-6 (eBook)

Library of Congress Control Number: 2021944038

Printed in the United States of America

24 25 26 27 28 29 30 / VP / 10 9 8 7 6 5 4 3 2

CONTENTS

Introduction

MY SOURDOUGH ADVENTURES

Sourdough has been a part of my life since I was a young girl. We lived near San Francisco and would often go into the city to Fisherman's Wharf on Sunday afternoons (before it became trendy—and crowded) to get live crabs and Boudin sourdough bread. A gigantic crab pot stood outside near the boat slips, and for a small fee, the person manning the pot would clean and cook our crabs for us. We'd buy several loaves of fresh sourdough bread and then rush home—riches in hand—and have a feast. Creamy butter thickly spread on slices of sourdough would assuage our hunger as we picked through the crab meat and made ourselves Crab Louie salads alongside more fresh bread. Those Sunday afternoons became a treasured memory for me, and the San Francisco sourdough bread, with its distinctive taste, was part of the gastronomic magic. Is it any wonder, then, that as an adult I wanted to recapture that magic?

Shortly after college, I began to actively pursue my varied interests, among them cooking and baking from scratch. In the back of my mind, I remembered the delicious bread of my youth and decided to try my hand at making sourdough. Times were different then, and try as I might, I couldn't lay my hands on an authentic San Francisco starter. While this obstacle may have slowed me down, it didn't stop me. I went to the local library (this was before the days of the internet) and began my research, and I soon had "recipes" to make my own starter. Long story short, my first attempts produced nothing but an off-smelling, pinkish mess that I knew wasn't right. So, for a time, I consoled myself with yeast bread baking.

Salvation came in the form of my brother, who had moved to Alaska. He was able to get an old Alaskan sourdough starter that the giver assured him was more than 100 years old, and my brother generously propagated a batch and gave it to me (which I brought home in my carry-on bag!). I was off and running, and that starter is still going strong 40 years later. Since then, I was able to buy a San Francisco sourdough starter (see Resources at the back of the book for links to purchasing your own), so now I keep two separate starters going, and I'm careful to never let them comingle.

Over the years, I've given away many batches of starter to folks wanting to begin their own sourdough adventure, and I've taught sourdough bread baking classes as well. And when my students take the first bite of their first loaf, their grins tell me I've helped yet another baker discover the thrill of taking flour, water, and salt and making mouthwatering treats for themselves and their loved ones. I hope the same will be said of you as well. So come along with me and discover for yourself the joy that is sourdough.

PART ONE

Getting Started

Chapter 1

WHAT IS SOURDOUGH, AND HOW DOES IT WORK?

*I*t's not known when sourdough as a leavening agent was first used, but sourdough yeast is well-documented in ancient Egypt, and the baked goods were used to feed the workers who built the pyramids. Also, the Old and New Testaments of the Bible contain numerous mentions of leavened and unleavened bread. (See, for instance, Exodus 34:25; Leviticus 7:12-14; Matthew 13:33; 1 Corinthians 5:6-7.) No one really knows how sourdough first came to be, but it's speculated that its discovery was accidental. Perhaps an ancient Egyptian forgot about their dough and when they returned, the loaf had risen and become lighter than usual. Not wishing to waste the precious ingredients, the dough was baked, and rudimentary sourdough was born. But even though its origins are steeped in mystery, the result has been with us for millennia. Until the development of commercial or baker's yeast in the 1800s, all leavened bread was made from wild yeasts—what we know as sourdough. But what exactly is sourdough yeast?

To get sourdough starter in its simplest form, flour and water are mixed together and left out at room temperature to ferment. Wild yeasts and bacteria begin to colonize on the flour and water mixture, and the mixture becomes more acidic. This in turn allows the sourdough-specific yeast and bacteria to take hold, and if all goes well, about a week later, a viable, stable starter has been produced. At this point, the baker can begin using the starter, remembering to always set a small portion aside to feed and let ferment for another day. It really is that simple.

Producing your own sourdough starter is easy, and the tools and supplies you'll need are surprisingly few. In the next chapter, I'll detail the absolute must-have tools you'll need to successfully make sourdough baked goods, as well as other tools that can make your job easier and more enjoyable. But trust me when I say that the tools needed are very few indeed—think of the Alaskan gold miners (the Alaskan "sour-doughs") or American pioneers on the arduous journey to the West. If they could do it, so can we.

Chapter 2

TOOLS AND SUPPLIES— COLLECTING WHAT YOU'LL NEED TO BEGIN

As I mentioned, the tools required to produce a delicious, airy loaf of sourdough bread are few indeed—flour, water, salt, a container for mixing and rising, and something to bake the bread in. That's it! But as with any endeavor, having a few more tools will make the job easier still.

Water

You can use tap water (although purists might beg to differ), but if you are on a well with a high mineral content, consider using bottled water instead. And if your municipal tap water contains chlorine, it's a good idea to let the water sit overnight so the chlorine has a chance to dissipate before you use it. But again—remember those pioneers and Alaskan gold miners. They did just fine using what they had available.

Flour

It's possible to use any grain-based flour to make or refresh your starter, but my experience has been that unbleached all-purpose white flour is the easiest to use for successful results. I refresh my established starters with unbleached white flour, and they are still going strong after many years. But that doesn't mean I never use other types of flours when sourdough baking. In fact, whole wheat flour makes a robust, hearty loaf that is hard to beat, and sourdough rye bread is heaven in a bite.

Salt

I generally use canning salt because I always have it on hand and it has no fillers, but a fine-ground sea salt works well also. Keep in mind that you want to use a smaller grind of salt so it can mix into the dough evenly, and read labels to ensure that you use non-iodized salt that is free of anticaking agents. Usually that means staying away from table salt.

Containers

You'll need something in which to mix and raise the dough, a storage container for keeping starter, and a baking vessel.

Mixing and raising bowl. Use glass or food-safe plastic for your containers and make sure there's enough room in the container to accommodate the risen dough. As an example, I use a half-gallon glass Pyrex bowl to mix and raise enough dough for one very large or two regular-sized loaves of bread. I rarely need to use something other than my trusty Pyrex as it seems a perfect size for most things.

Baking vessel. Cast iron is king—at least when it comes to sourdough. I use a well-seasoned cast-iron Dutch oven that has a flat cast-iron lid, because when I get ready to bake, I put the loaf inside the lid, flip the Dutch oven upside down, and place it on top. I use cast iron because it's thick and can take high heat, and once the lid is on, it keeps the steam from the dough inside the pot. This moisture helps the bread to rise better at the beginning of baking, producing those large holes that sourdough is known for, and makes for a chewy crust and moist interior.

Storage jar for storing starter. I use a wide-mouth quart canning jar to refresh and store my starter in the refrigerator between baking sessions. I don't use a lid when storing my starter. Instead, I place a piece of plastic wrap over the top of the jar and use a thick rubber band to hold the plastic in place and keep out unwanted wild yeasts and bacteria.

Other Tools to Make the Job Easier

"Other tools" sounds innocent enough, doesn't it? But oh, the possibilities! Here are some of my favorites.

Digital food scale. You can successfully make sourdough products by measure versus weight, but a digital scale makes such a difference in the end. I resisted using a scale for some time, but now I always weigh my ingredients, at least when making bread. I've found that my baking turns out more consistent, and I can replicate a recipe with no surprises. Find a digital scale that has a tare weight feature (the ability to subtract the weight of a container before adding your ingredients) and gives the weight in ounces, grams, milliliters, kilos, pounds, and so on. You'll find that many baking recipes use grams as the weight of choice.

Dough scraper. Also called a bench scraper or bench knife, this is very handy to have around when you are moving or forming your dough. I have two: a metal one that is squared off and one made of pliable silicone that is crescent shaped to accommodate the curve of a bowl.

Linen cloth or couche. Floured linen cloth is perfect when you want to rise free-form loaves such as baguettes. A baker's couche works even better, but a linen cloth will suffice and is usually cheaper. Some folks use fine-weave kitchen towels, and when liberally floured, they work just fine.

Banneton. Bannetons—otherwise known as proofing baskets—are made from natural rattan and come in various sizes and shapes. They also give a lovely look to the finished loaf. I admit to collecting bannetons. They give my bread a professional look.

Proofing box. If you search online for a folding bread proofer/yogurt maker (they're electric), you'll find these. They are especially useful when your home is on the cool side, and I use mine in the winter months. I have a Brød & Taylor and recommend the product, but just be sure that whichever proofing box you purchase will be large enough for your bread baking needs.

Lame. A lame is the baker's answer to a sharp knife. Lames have handles that hold a double-edged razor blade. You use them to cut into the top of the loaf right before baking (called slashing); the cut areas help to release bubbles and produce the spring that is a desirable feature of sourdough bread.

Chapter 3

SOURDOUGH STARTERS– TWO WAYS TO GET STARTED

Before you can begin turning out delicious sourdough baking, you need a viable starter. Starters are the foundation for all your sourdough baking, and owning a good one is a joy. I always keep two starters going. My authentic San Francisco starter is special to me because it brings back such good memories of my childhood. But my Alaskan starter is my favorite because it comes from a starter that began approximately 150 years ago. I admit to bragging about my starters on occasion! But the truth is, a new starter can be just as wonderful. All you need to do is tend it at regular intervals, and soon you'll have a lively starter of your own.

There are two ways to begin.

Capturing Wild Yeast

Wild Yeast Starter

Gather your tools: a clean wide-mouth quart canning jar or other suitable container, flour, water that is room temperature or slightly tepid (if you have chlorinated water, such as municipal tap water, let the water sit in a clean, uncovered container overnight

to dissipate the chlorine before using), and a stainless-steel spoon or rubber or silicone spatula for mixing. (I use the larger stainless-steel soup spoons that came with my flatware set.)

Days 1, 2, and 3 (morning and evening, about 12 hours apart). In the canning jar, add ½ cup flour (if you use fresh whole wheat flour, the whole grains will kickstart the fermenting process, but it's not necessary) and ½ cup water; stir to mix well. Cover the jar with something breathable, such as a coffee filter, paper towel, or cloth napkin, and hold in place with a rubber band. Leave the mixture on the counter at room temperature (70 to 72°). After 12 hours, add another ½ cup flour and ½ cup water; stir well to mix. Repeat this process every 12 hours on days 2 and 3, adding the same amounts in the jar each time.

Days 4, 5, and 6. The 12-hour feeding schedule and the amount of flour and water stay the same, but beginning on day 4, discard all but ½ cup of the starter before feeding each time. This is so the starter doesn't overflow the jar. Also, on about day 4 you will notice some activity—bubbles will begin to form in the starter, and it might increase slightly in volume and develop a slightly sour smell.

Day 7 and beyond. Beginning with day 7, reduce the feeding to once a day, continuing to discard all but ½ cup of the starter before feeding. At approximately day 7, your starter is ready to use. It will smell sour, have lots of bubbles, and rise to nearly double in 4 to 8 hours, although it could take longer if your home is on the cool side.

If you won't be using your starter now, you can cover the jar once the starter is active, risen, and bubbly and store it in the refrigerator. (I use plastic wrap with a rubber band to hold the plastic in place.) It can stay viable for many weeks in the refrigerator, but it's best to feed your starter every week or so. See chapter 4 for how to keep a starter fed.

Sourdough has enjoyed a resurgence, and you probably know someone who is a sourdough baker.

Using Active Dry Yeast to Help Get a Starter Going

Start by gathering your ingredients:

2 cups warm, unchlorinated water (if you have chlorinated water, such as municipal tap water, let the water sit in a clean, uncovered container overnight to dissipate the chlorine before using)

2¼ tsp. (1 package) active dry yeast

2 cups unbleached white flour, whole wheat flour, or a combination of the two

Pour the yeast into the water, stirring with a wooden spoon until it's completely dissolved. Add the flour and stir again until the mixture is smooth. Cover the jar with something breathable, such as a coffee filter, paper towel, or cloth napkin, and hold in place with a rubber band.

Set the covered container on the counter at room temperature for 5 to 7 days, stirring the mixture once a day. At the end of this time, the mixture should have risen and become bubbly and frothy. At this point, you can use it or set it in the refrigerator for use at a later time. Or you can keep it on the counter, but if you do, you'll need to feed the starter every day. See chapter 4 to learn how to maintain an established or neglected starter.

Obtaining an Established Starter

Obtaining an established starter is far easier than trying to capture wild yeast, and the results are almost always guaranteed, which is why I recommend this method.

Get a starter from a friend. When I first began baking with sourdough, it was almost impossible to find someone with an active starter they could share with me. My brother's gift of the Alaskan starter seemed like a rare treasure, and I was ecstatic to receive it. I guarded that starter anxiously at first, knowing that I'd have a hard time replacing it if things went wrong. Today, sourdough has enjoyed a resurgence, and you probably know someone who is a sourdough baker. If so, ask them if they would be amenable to giving you your own starter. They'll likely know what to do, and you'll be in business in short order.

Buy a sourdough starter. Another way to get a starter is to simply go online and buy one. How easy is that? And to make things more interesting, you'll find some unique starters to whet your interest. Some starters come in liquid form, but I suggest buying the dehydrated packets. It will still take about a week before the starter is lively enough to use, but the results are almost foolproof. Check out the resources on page 173 for online stores that sell starters.

Chapter 4

MAINTAINING, STORING, AND RESTORING YOUR STARTER

*I*n days past, maintaining your sourdough starter would have been one of the most important items on your chore list. Store-bought yeast wasn't always available or affordable. Today, of course, most of us can easily buy yeast or another sourdough starter with no worries. But maintaining your established starter is easy, and an aged, healthy starter has a deep, lively flavor that can't be matched. So to me, the decision is simple: Maintain your starter and reap the benefits.

Maintaining an Established Starter

How often should you feed your starter? The answer depends on your storage method. If your starter sits on a counter, you'll want to feed it daily (or at least every other day). If you refrigerate your starter, feeding it once every week or two will keep it happy, although it can last in the fridge for as long as two months. If you store your starter in the freezer, it can last up to a year between feedings if it doesn't succumb to freezer burn. And if you decide to dry your starter, it can last six months on a cupboard shelf, two years in the refrigerator, or indefinitely in the freezer.

The next point to be made is that you can feed and refresh your starter with as much or as little water and flour as you want (within reason). If you are simply refreshing your starter prior to putting it back in the refrigerator, a smaller amount is more economical. But if you plan on making two large loaves of bread, for example, you'll obviously need to use more. Here's the recipe for feeding/refreshing your starter:

Starter Refresh by Measure

½ cup slightly tepid water (if you have chlorinated water such as municipal tap water, let the water sit in a clean, uncovered container overnight to dissipate the chlorine before using)

½ cup flour of your choice (I use all-purpose white flour and use other flours only at baking time)

1 to 2 T. old starter to "seed" the mixture

In a clean jar or bowl, thoroughly mix all the ingredients. Cover with plastic wrap and allow to sit on the counter until the starter has awakened; the starter should be bubbly and have risen. This could take up to 12 hours, especially if it's been a while since you last refreshed. I use a wide-mouth quart canning jar and mix the starter in the evening so it can rise on the kitchen counter (at room temperature) overnight.

Starter Refresh by Weight

125 grams slightly tepid water (if you have chlorinated water such as municipal tap water, let the water sit in a clean, uncovered container overnight to dissipate the chlorine before using)

125 grams flour of your choice (I use all-purpose white flour and use other flours only at baking time)

1 to 2 T. old starter to "seed" the mixture

In a clean jar or bowl, thoroughly mix all the ingredients. Cover with plastic wrap and allow to sit on the counter until the starter has awakened; the starter should be bubbly and have risen. This could take up to 12 hours, especially if it's been a while since it was refreshed. Making the starter in the evening works well—simply let it rest at room temperature overnight, and in the morning it will be perfect.

Note: Weighing your starter ingredients versus measuring them is the best way to maintain a consistent starter, and it's my method of choice.

Active Versus Discard Starter

- *Active starter* is bubbly and doubled in volume. Generally, this comes about 8 to 12 hours after the last feeding. Active starter is used most often when you want your product to rise well.

- *Discard starter* is active starter that has gone beyond its highest volume. Discard starter loses much of its volume as the air bubbles pop and it becomes smoother and thinner. Discard starter is most often used for quick-and-easy recipes that don't need much rising time.

Storing Your Starter

There will be times when you won't use your sourdough starter every day or two, and quite possibly for longer periods of time. But there's no need to throw away your precious starter. You can successfully store it so it's available when you are once again ready to bake sourdough goodies.

Refrigerating Your Starter

If you choose to store your starter in the fridge, you'll only need to refresh it every week or two. But really, you can store it for much longer between feedings. I've stored mine for six or seven weeks with no adverse effects, although I sometimes choose to do two refreshes in a row before putting it back into storage. This helps to keep the yeast livelier. Place your refreshed starter (starter that has about doubled in volume) in the coldest part of your refrigerator, covered with plastic wrap and secured with a rubber band. When ready to use, place the container on your kitchen counter and allow it to come to room temperature before using.

Freezing Your Starter

Frozen starter can last a year between feedings if it doesn't get freezer burn. To prevent burning, take care to remove all oxygen from the starter container. I use heavy-duty quart-sized freezer bags and spoon or pour my starter into the bag. Then I carefully press the bag to remove the air. Once I'm confident there's no more air inside the bag, I seal it up and then place the bag inside a second bag before storing. When ready to use, place the frozen starter (still in the bag) into a bowl on the counter and allow it to come to room temperature.

Drying Your Starter

Make a note of how much starter you plan to dehydrate. It's best if you weigh the amount. Spread the sourdough starter in a *very* thin layer on parchment paper. Place the starter into a dehydrator at 95°. Alternatively, you can place the parchment paper with the starter in the oven with the oven light turned on. Leave the starter until it's thoroughly dry on top; peel the starter from the plastic or paper, turn it over, place it back on the plastic wrap or paper, and thoroughly dry the other side. Continue turning and drying the starter until it's *extremely* dry and brittle. Allow the dehydrated starter to cool completely; break into pieces and then pulverize the starter using a blender or food processor.

Weighing your starter ingredients versus measuring them is the best way to maintain consistency.

Place the pulverized starter in a heavy-duty food-grade bag and remove as much air as you can. Mark the package with the original liquid equivalent of the now-dehydrated starter, because when you rehydrate it, you'll want to

use that same weight measurement to determine how much water to add. And when you do rehydrate the dried starter, you may need to refresh it several times before it becomes active and lively.

Maintaining a Neglected Starter

If a starter has been neglected, it will drop in volume (because of the loss of bubbles) and become thinner and smoother. And if it's left long enough, "hooch" will likely collect on top of the starter. Hooch is a dark brownish-gray opaque liquid that appears on top when the starter has eaten all the food that is available. This means starvation and ultimately death for the starter, so now is the time to feed your starter. I pour off the hooch and stir the contents before using the starter to "seed" a new batch. Follow the directions above for either **Starter Refresh by Measure** or **Starter Refresh by Weight**. The new batch of starter will become bubbly, but once it nearly doubles in height in the jar, follow the starter refresh directions once more to make a new batch. This new batch should become livelier than the first batch and take less time to double in bulk, and you can begin baking with the starter or store it for use another time.

How to Tell if Your Starter Has Gone Bad

It's surprising just how hard it is to kill an established sourdough starter. Even when it is neglected, with judicious feeding, you'll be able to save a starter. True, it may be sluggish at first, taking longer to bubble and rise, but with another feeding or two, your starter will become lively once again, ready to use in recipes. So how do you know if your starter is truly beyond saving?

We've already discussed hooch, but I'll do a quick repeat. Hooch develops on a starter when it's been neglected and doesn't have much more to feed on. Hooch is a grayish-brownish opaque liquid that sits on top of the starter. If your starter develops hooch, pour off the liquid and then feed/refresh your starter immediately. It needs food…right now. Even when hooch develops, your starter hasn't gone bad, and it can be saved.

Note: If you see a furry coating on any part of your starter or hooch, this indicates mold is present, and your starter must be discarded. If you observe pink or orange streaks or spots on the top of your starter or hooch, these also indicate that mold has infiltrated your starter, and it's time to discard all of it and begin anew.

Heat will kill your starter as well. Yeast dies at about 140°, but your starter can die at lower temperatures than that. The rule of thumb is to never let your starter get too hot—70° is ideal, but during the summer your kitchen very well could be hotter than that by as much as 10°. Your starter should be fine even then, but you'll notice that it will rise and bubble much faster than it would on a cold winter morning. If you are experiencing severe hot weather and don't have air-conditioning, it's a good idea to store your starter in the refrigerator and only pull it out to feed it or when you want to bake something.

Neglect your starter long enough and it *will* die. But keep in mind that sourdough is amazingly resilient.

Chapter 5

MEASURING VERSUS WEIGHING THE INGREDIENTS

*I*f you live in the United States, chances are you *measure* your ingredients (ounces, cups, and so on). However, if you live in, say, Europe, you likely *weigh* your ingredients instead (grams, milliliters, kilograms, and the like). You may be wondering if one method is better than the other, and the answer is yes, at least when you're baking something.

Consider flour. The standard measure for a cup of all-purpose flour is 4½ ounces. But depending on the way you put the flour into your measuring cup and how old the flour is, you could mismeasure by an ounce or more. When baking, that can make the difference between a chewy cookie and one that's flat and crisp. Or producing a dry loaf of sourdough bread. When measuring by weight, a cup of all-purpose flour is always 120 grams—there are never any surprises.

Use a Food Scale
If you grew up measuring all ingredients like I did, you may resist using a food scale. For the longest time, I shied away from weighing ingredients. But I finally capitulated and am so glad I did. My baking—especially my sourdough breads—are so much

better now, and because I weigh my ingredients, I know exactly what my end products will look and taste like every single time. It's also much easier to scale a favorite recipe up or down depending on how much I want to make. So if you are a measurer, be courageous and run right out and buy a food scale. The difference will be noticeable, and you'll be so glad you did.

But what if you find a recipe that you'd like to try that uses the type of measurement you don't normally use? This shouldn't pose a problem because it's easy to change the way you're measuring with a bit of simple math. Here are a few guidelines that might help:

A Guide to Weighing and Measuring Ingredients

1 cup all-purpose or bread flour = 120 grams

1 cup whole wheat flour = 125 grams

1 cup granulated sugar = 200 grams

1 cup (packed) brown sugar = 220 grams

1 cup water = 240 grams

1 cup milk = 240 grams

1 teaspoon salt = 6 grams

1 teaspoon baking powder = 4 grams

1 teaspoon baking soda = 6 grams

½ stick butter (4 tablespoons) = 113 grams

1000 grams = 1 kilogram

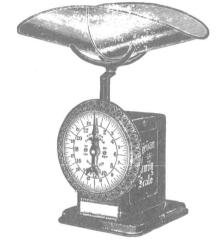

You'll find recipes in this book that use weights as well as measures. But don't let that stop you from trying a recipe. Follow it as written or use the handy guide above to help convert your ingredients.

In my experience, I pretty much always use weights when baking bread, and I go back and forth between weighing and measuring for other baked goods.

Chapter 6

A BASIC SOURDOUGH LOAF—THE PROCESS

Y ou've gotten your starter, either as a gift from a fellow baker, by catching wild yeast and making your own, or by purchasing some. You've worked with your starter, and now it's lively and ready to use. This chapter will show you how to make your first loaf of sourdough bread so you can begin to get a feel for the process.

Keep several things in mind:

The following instructions are not set in stone. Your results will no doubt vary because no two starters are exactly alike, and room temperature isn't always consistent. So if an instruction says, for instance, to let the dough rise until almost doubled, it could take as little as 3 or 4 hours, or it could take 8 hours or even more. You can help along a cold environment by using a proofing box that allows you to set a perfect temperature, and you can always place your dough in the refrigerator for as long as several days to slow down the process. In general, the slower your dough rises, the sourer it will be. So once you're comfortable with the process, you can change things up by using temperature to get exactly the taste you desire. Or if you'll be away from home for some reason, you can place the dough in the refrigerator until you return.

Just remember that when you take the dough out of the refrigerator, it will need some time to get to room temperature and begin rising again.

A Basic Sourdough Bread Loaf

This recipe makes a small, ½ kg. loaf. You will refer to this Basic Sourdough Bread Loaf recipe throughout this book because the process is the same for many of the following recipes.

The Morning of the Day Before You Plan to Bake

Pull out your saved starter and make two new batches.

Starter to save for later. Combine these items (in this order) in a clean quart canning jar or other container and mix thoroughly.

125 g. tepid water

125 g. unbleached all-purpose flour

1 to 2 T. saved starter

Cover the jar with plastic wrap and leave it on the counter until it is fully active and has formed bubbles and foam. This could take from 3 to 12 hours. Place the starter in the refrigerator—this is your saved starter, to be stored for use on another day's baking.

Starter to use in this recipe. Combine these items (in this order) in a large container, such as a half-gallon Pyrex bowl, and mix thoroughly.

100 g. tepid water

100 g. flour

1 to 2 T. saved starter

Cover the bowl with plastic wrap and leave it on the counter until it is active and has formed bubbles and foam. This could take from 2 to 8 hours. This container of mature starter is what you will use to make the bread.

Note: The amount of flour and water will vary depending on how much mature starter you need for a recipe. The amounts listed above make 200 g. of active starter, which is enough to make this loaf recipe.

The Afternoon or Early Evening of the Day Before You Plan to Bake

Follow these instructions to make the dough and knead it.

200 g. active starter that you just made (see the instructions on page 26)

400 g. all-purpose or bread flour

200 g. water

10 g. salt

Add the flour and water to the large container that has the active starter you made earlier in the day. Mix well. I begin mixing by using a large stainless-steel spoon (you can also use a wooden spoon or silicone spatula) and then finish up mixing by hand. At this point, the mixture will be shaggy and won't stay together very well—this is normal. Cover the container with plastic wrap or a clean towel (I use plastic wrap because it helps to preserve the moisture in the dough) and let it sit on the counter for 30 to 45 minutes. This step *autolyzes* the dough, which is a baker's term that means letting the dough rest for a while so all the liquid is absorbed and fully hydrates the flour. Next, add the salt and knead the dough to mix it throughout.

Note: Full disclosure here. I sometimes add the salt to the flour when I am first mixing the dough. Why? Because I can't tell you how many times I forgot to add it later. Does it seem to make a difference? Not that I've noticed.

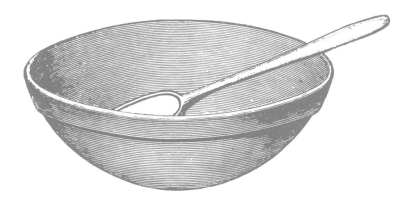

Use the stretch and fold method to knead the dough.

1. If the dough is very sticky (and it will be!), you can run your hands quickly through water before you begin or dust a bit of flour on your fingers. Make a fist with one hand and press your knuckles gently on the center top of the dough; with your other hand, grab an edge on the underneath side of the dough along the side of the bowl and lift the dough up, gently pressing with your fisted hand to keep the dough in the bowl as you lift from the sides. You won't be able to lift very far before the dough tears, which is completely normal at this point. Press the bit of dough you just stretched back into the top center.

2. Now turn the bowl a quarter of a turn and lift up the next edge of dough, knuckles on the center top of the dough to keep it in the bowl, stretching until it begins to tear, and then lay the dough on top. Continue through all four "sides" and then cover the bowl with the plastic wrap and allow the dough to rest for about 30 minutes.

3. Stretch and fold the dough six times—once every 30 minutes. You will soon notice that the dough stays together, has a smooth and satiny sheen, and gets quite thin when stretched before tearing. Your dough is working! The number of times you stretch and fold isn't critical, and with practice you'll learn when your dough is ready. And if you get busy and forget to stretch and fold your dough at 30-minute intervals, it's not a problem. Just keep doing the sets of stretches and folds for a total of about six times.

Cover the dough in the container with plastic wrap and let it sit on the counter to rise (some people call this the *bulk proof* stage) overnight. I make sure to tent the plastic so there's plenty of room for the dough to rise, and I secure the plastic with a large rubber band or piece of string tied around the edge of the bowl.

If it's a hot summer day and your kitchen is warm, you can set the covered bowl in the refrigerator overnight to keep the dough from overproofing. Simply remove the dough from the refrigerator in the morning and let it sit at room temperature until it's nearly doubled in bulk and then continue.

The number of times you stretch and fold isn't critical, and with practice you'll learn when your dough is ready.

The Morning of Baking Day

Follow these instructions to make the bread.

Note: Your dough has greatly increased, and the overnight fermentation has boosted the number of organisms in the dough, producing a lively culture that allows the flavor to develop.

Gently turn out the dough onto a floured work surface, cover the dough, and let it rest for about 30 minutes. You want to treat the dough gently to retain as many air bubbles as possible.

Next you will shape the dough.

- If you plan on baking a **round loaf**, grab the side of the dough farthest from you and pull it toward the center. Continue this around the dough to form a ball; pinch the edges of the segments together at the center. The surface of the dough on the underside is now round and smooth and the top is seamed. Now it's time to move the shaped loaf into a willow proofing basket (a banneton) or bowl with the seam-side up. Dust the loaf with flour before placing it in the basket or bowl. This is where your bench scraper comes in handy—slide it underneath the dough and move it into the baking container. Cover the dough, and proof it until it's about doubled in bulk, approximately 2 to 4 hours.

  If you don't have a banneton or suitable bowl, you can use parchment paper that's been lightly floured to hold the dough. Form the dough into a ball as explained above and then carefully turn the round over so the seam side is down. Cup your hands around the sides of the dough and gently scoop the dough under the round, creating a tight surface on the ball of dough. When you're ready to bake the bread, all you have to do is lift the dough, still on the parchment paper, and set it on your baking sheet to bake.

- If you plan on using a **loaf pan**, continue to further shape the dough to a size that fits the pan. Dust the loaf with flour, set it into a loaf pan seam-side down, and cover and proof it until it's about doubled in bulk, approximately 2 to 4 hours.

- For a **baguette** or **French loaf**, continue to further shape the loaf by rolling the dough to lengthen it. Dust the loaf with flour, set it on a parchment paper–lined baking sheet, cover, and proof it until it's about doubled in bulk, approximately 2 to 4 hours.

If you notice that your loaf spreads out more than just from bulking up, chances are you need to add a bit more flour. Knead in a small amount, loaf up the dough again, and let it rise until nearly doubled in bulk.

Slashing the Loaf

Slashing the surface of the dough immediately before baking accomplishes several things. Slashing patterns provide an attractive appearance on the crust, and many bakers have slashing "signatures" they use again and again to identify a loaf as having come from their kitchen or having a certain flavor. Slashing also allows an escape

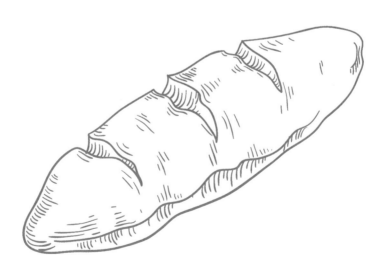

route for expanding gases during baking. This makes the bread noticeably expand or "spring," and the slashed patterns stand out beautifully.

Razor blades or lames are ideal for slashing. Just make sure the blade is very sharp so it cuts instead of tears the dough. Allowing the dough to dry briefly before slashing helps as well. Make the cuts at about a 45-degree angle, between ¼ inch and ½ inch deep.

Be patient and practice your cuts. It takes repetition to make a good-looking crust.

You want to treat the dough gently to retain as many air bubbles as possible.

Baking Your Bread

- If you plan on baking a round, baguette, or French loaf, place a baking stone on your oven rack to hold the loaf while baking.

- For a traditional chewy crust, supply steam during baking by placing a pan of boiling water below the rack that will hold the loaf, or spritz the wall of the oven—not the bread itself—every 5 minutes for the first 15 minutes of bake time.

- For a softer crust, brush the loaf with melted butter or oil before baking.

If you decide to bake your bread in a cast-iron Dutch oven or roaster, place the loaf onto the lid of the Dutch oven and use the pot itself for the cover. Preheat the Dutch oven before placing the loaf inside. But remember—the cast iron is hot, so use oven mitts. Leave the pot on for the first 20 minutes of baking and then remove it to finish baking.

Here are two methods for baking your bread:

1. Set your bread in a cold oven without covering it. Turn on the oven to 375°, place the loaf in the center of the oven, and bake for about 70 minutes, or until the bread has a brown crust and sounds a bit hollow when thumped. Begin spritzing the oven walls with water as soon as the oven comes up to temperature. Spritz every 5 minutes for a total of about 15 minutes.

2. Preheat the oven to 400 to 450°. Place the loaf in the center of the oven and bake for 40 to 50 minutes or until the bread has a brown crust and sounds a bit

hollow when thumped. Here, too, you can use the steam from water during the first 15 minutes of baking if desired.

Note: Why the broad range in temperatures? Bakers have different opinions as to how dark sourdough bread should be. In general, the higher the temperature, the darker the loaf will be. You'll soon decide how dark you like your crust.

When the bread is finished baking, promptly remove it from the baking sheet or loaf pan and set the loaf on a wire rack to cool. Even though you'll be sorely tempted, don't slice into the bread for at least 20 minutes. The resulting lofty texture and lovely sourdough "holes" are well worth the wait.

PART TWO

Recipes

Chapter 7

CLASSIC SOURDOUGH BREADS

For many people, the holy grail of sourdough is baking the classic bread. I certainly thought that when I started out. My one aim was to tackle the mysteries of flour, water, and salt and successfully produce the sourdough bread of my youth. After a bit of trial and error, I found success, and as I gained experience, I found joy in the process. I hope the same for you.

The choices to be found in this section are numerous, but all of them share one thing in common: Sourdough bread is uncommonly delicious, so start by making a few loaves of Matthew's White Bread. When you feel confident, move on to some of the other recipes. Cheesy Jalapeño Bread or Roasted Garlic Bread are good choices to spread your baking wings. Or maybe the thought of something hearty piques your interest? Then be sure to try the whole wheat or rye bread recipes. Whichever recipes you choose, take time to savor the process and delight in the taste. After all, it's fresh, homemade, and best of all, your creation.

Caramelized Onion Bread

(Refer to A Basic Sourdough Bread Loaf on page 26 for instructions and techniques.)

Caramelized onions

1 T. olive oil (a bit more if needed)

½ large onion, chopped into small pieces

¼ tsp. granulated sugar

¼ tsp. salt

Bread dough

533 g. unbleached all-purpose flour

267 g. active starter

267 g. water

13 g. salt

Caramelized onions from the recipe above

In a medium skillet, heat the oil on medium heat. Add the onion and stir to coat the pieces with oil. Add the sugar and salt and cook, stirring so the onion pieces don't burn, until the onions have softened and turned a light golden brown (about 20 minutes). If the onions seem to get dry, you can add a small amount of oil to keep them from sticking to the pan and burning. When done, transfer the caramelized onions to a small container and refrigerate them until needed.

In a large bowl, combine all the ingredients except the salt and caramelized onions. Cover the bowl with plastic wrap and let the dough sit at room temperature for about 30 minutes. Sprinkle the salt throughout the dough and mix well again to fully incorporate the salt. Keeping the dough in the container, stretch and fold the dough 3 times, covering the bowl with plastic wrap and letting the dough rest for 30 minutes between sessions each time. After the third stretch and fold session, cover the dough and allow it to rest for 30 minutes. Then add the caramelized onions, kneading gently to begin mixing the pieces throughout the dough. Perform 3 more stretch and folds 30 minutes apart, covering the bowl between sessions.

Keeping the bowl covered with plastic wrap, let the dough rise until about doubled, usually 4 to 8 hours or overnight.

Gently turn the dough out onto a floured work surface and shape it. Cover with plastic wrap and let rise for about 4 hours or until almost doubled.

Slash the top. Preheat the oven to 400 to 450° and bake for 45 to 50 minutes or until done.

Makes 1 loaf

Cheesy Jalapeño Bread

(Refer to A Basic Sourdough Bread Loaf on page 26 for instructions and techniques.)

Starter

50 g. unbleached all-purpose flour

50 g. water

15 g. starter

Bread dough

Starter made the night before

360 g. water

500 g. unbleached all-purpose flour, or a combination of whole wheat and all-purpose flours

10 g. salt

50 g. sliced jalapeño peppers (fresh, roasted, or pickled)

100 g. sharp cheddar cheese, shredded

The night before:

In the large mixing bowl you plan to make the bread dough in, mix the starter ingredients; cover with plastic wrap and let the starter sit at room temperature overnight.

The next morning:

In the bowl that contains the prepared starter, add the water and stir to combine. Whisk the flour and salt together and add to the starter, mixing with your hands and working until there are no dry bits of flour. (I like to mix in about half the flour mixture with a large spoon and then add the remaining flour mixture and mix by hand.) Cover the bowl with plastic wrap and let the dough rest at room temperature for 2 hours.

Perform 2 sets of stretch and folds 30 minutes apart, and cover the bowl when the dough is resting. After the second stretch, fold, and rest period, add the jalapeño peppers and cheese and stretch and fold 3 to 4 more times at 30-minute intervals, covering the bowl each time. After the last stretch and fold, cover the bowl and let the dough rise for 2 to 3 hours.

Turn the dough out onto a floured work surface and shape the dough into a circle or oblong. Flour the outside of the dough, cover it, and let it rise at room temperature for about 3 hours.

Preheat the oven to 450°. If using a Dutch oven or similar bread baker, place the baking dish into the oven to also preheat.

Slash the top of the loaf with a razor or lame and then carefully place the loaf into the preheated Dutch oven. (I use the lid for my base and the Dutch oven itself for the cover as it's much easier to get the loaf situated.)

Bake covered for 30 minutes; remove the top and continue baking for an additional 20 to 25 minutes. If using a baking stone or sheet, place a pan of boiling water in the oven on a rack under the bread to add steam to the baking. Remove the bread from the Dutch oven and set it on a wire rack to cool before slicing.

Makes 1 loaf

Cranberry Pecan Bread

(Refer to A Basic Sourdough Bread Loaf on page 26 for instructions and techniques.)

200 g. unbleached all-purpose flour

200 g. whole wheat flour

20 g. pecan pieces

20 g. dried cranberries

10 g. salt

200 g. active starter

225 g. water

In a medium mixing bowl, stir together the flours, pecan pieces, dried cranberries, and salt. Add the remaining ingredients, mix to combine, and then let the dough sit for about 30 minutes. Keeping the dough in the container, stretch and fold the dough about 6 times at 30-minute intervals. At first, the inclusions will tend to fall out, but use your fingers to press them gently into the dough as you stretch and fold. As you continue the stretch and fold sessions, the pecans and cranberries will become evenly incorporated throughout. Cover the bowl and let the dough rise until about doubled, usually 4 to 8 hours or overnight.

Gently turn out the dough onto a floured work surface and shape it. Cover and let rise for about 4 hours or until nicely risen.

Slash the top. Preheat the oven to 400 to 450° and bake for 40 to 50 minutes or until done. Cool on a wire rack.

Makes 1 loaf

Fifty/Fifty White and Wheat Bread

(Refer to A Basic Sourdough Bread Loaf on page 26 for instructions and techniques.)

225 g. water

200 g. active starter

200 g. unbleached all-purpose flour

200 g. whole wheat flour

10 g. salt

In a large bowl, mix all ingredients except the salt. Cover the bowl with plastic wrap and let the dough sit at room temperature for about 30 minutes. Sprinkle the salt over the dough and mix well again to fully incorporate the salt throughout. Keeping the dough in the container, stretch and fold the dough about 6 times at 30-minute intervals, covering the bowl with plastic wrap each time. Keeping the bowl covered with plastic wrap, let the dough rise until about doubled, usually 4 to 8 hours or overnight.

Gently turn out the dough onto a floured work surface and shape it. Cover with plastic wrap and let rise about 4 hours or until about doubled.

Slash the top. Preheat the oven to 400 to 450° and bake for 45 to 55 minutes or until done. Cool on a wire rack.

Makes 1 loaf

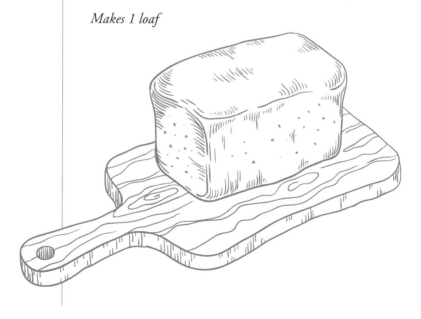

Fifty/Fifty White and Wheat Bread II

(Refer to A Basic Sourdough Loaf on page 26 for instructions and techniques.)

450 g. water

400 g. active starter

400 g. unbleached all-purpose flour

50 g. whole wheat flour

20 g. salt

In a large bowl, mix all ingredients except the salt. Cover the bowl with plastic wrap and let the dough sit at room temperature for about 30 minutes; sprinkle the salt over the dough and mix well again to fully incorporate the salt throughout. Keeping the dough in the container, stretch and fold the dough every 30 minutes or so about 6 times, covering the bowl with plastic wrap each time. Keeping the bowl covered with plastic wrap, let the dough rise until about doubled, usually 4 to 8 hours or overnight.

Gently turn out the dough onto a floured work surface and shape it. Cover the loaf with plastic wrap and let rise for 2 to 4 hours or until about doubled.

Slash the top. Preheat the oven to 400 to 450° and bake for 45 to 55 minutes or until done. Cool on a wire rack.

Makes 1 large or 2 small loaves

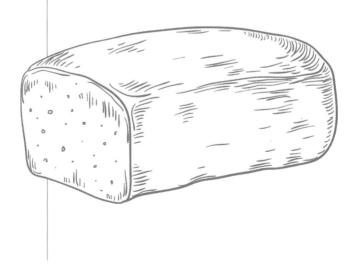

Gruyère Cheese Bread

(Refer to A Basic Sourdough Bread Loaf on page 26 for instructions and techniques.)

300 g. water

267 g. active starter

267 g. unbleached all-purpose flour

267 g. whole wheat flour

13 g. salt

50 g. Gruyère cheese, shredded

In a large bowl, mix all the ingredients except the salt and Gruyére cheese. Cover the bowl with plastic wrap and let the dough sit at room temperature for about 30 minutes. Sprinkle the salt over the dough and mix well again to fully incorporate the salt throughout. Cover the dough and let it rest for 30 minutes.

Keeping the dough in the container, stretch and fold the dough every 30 minutes. Do this 3 times, covering the bowl with plastic wrap after each session.

Add the Gruyére cheese, doing your best to mix it throughout the dough. Stretch and fold the dough 3 more times (for a total of 6 times), covering the bowl with plastic wrap after each session.

Keeping the bowl covered with plastic wrap, let the dough rise until about doubled, usually from 4 to 8 hours or overnight.

Gently turn out the dough onto a floured work surface and shape it. Cover the loaf with plastic wrap and let rise for 2 to 4 hours or until risen by at least half.

Slash the top. Preheat the oven to 400 to 450° and bake for 45 to 55 minutes or until done. Cool on a wire rack.

Makes 1 loaf

Italian Herb Bread

(Refer to A Basic Sourdough Bread Loaf on page 26 for instructions and techniques.)

240 g. active starter

15 g. butter

240 g. milk

1 tsp. salt

1 tsp. granulated sugar

½ tsp. dried thyme

½ tsp. dried oregano

½ tsp. dried basil

490 g. unbleached all-purpose flour

The night before:

In a large mixing bowl, add the starter. Melt the butter in a microwaveable bowl that's large enough to also hold the milk; microwave until the butter is completed melted. Pour the milk into the bowl that contains the melted butter and then add the salt, sugar, thyme, oregano, and basil. Mix well. Check to see that the milk mixture is no hotter than 100°; when cool enough, pour it into the bowl that contains the starter and mix well again. Add the flour one cup at a time and mix after each addition. When the dough becomes too stiff to mix by hand, turn out onto a floured work surface and knead it, adding flour as you go along, until the dough is smooth and satiny. This will take 8 or more minutes. Place the dough back into a clean mixing bowl. Cover the bowl with plastic wrap and let it rise at room temperature overnight. The next morning, the dough should be about doubled in bulk.

The next morning:

Gently turn out the dough onto a floured work surface and allow it to rest for 30 minutes. Shape the dough into the shape you want. Place the loaf either onto a baking sheet lined with parchment paper, onto a silicone baking mat, or into a greased loaf pan. Let it rise at room temperature for 2 to 4 hours or until the loaf doubles in size (if a loaf pan is used, let it rise to the top of the loaf pan).

You can bake the bread two ways:

- Place the pan into a cool oven and then turn the oven to 375°. Bake for 70 minutes.

- Preheat the oven to 450° and bake the bread for 40 to 45 minutes.

Remove the bread from the oven (or loaf pan) and place it on a wire rack to cool.

Makes 1 loaf

Matthew's Semolina Bread

(Refer to A Basic Sourdough Bread Loaf on page 26 for instructions and techniques.)

300 g. unbleached all-purpose flour

225 g. water

200 g. active starter

100 g. semolina flour

10 g. salt

In a large bowl, mix all the ingredients except the salt. Cover the bowl with plastic wrap and let the dough sit at room temperature for about 30 minutes. Sprinkle the salt over the dough and mix well again to fully incorporate the salt throughout. Keeping the dough in the container, stretch and fold the dough every 30 minutes or so, about 5 or 6 times, covering the bowl with plastic wrap each time. Cover the bowl and let the dough rise until about doubled, usually 4 to 8 hours or overnight.

Gently turn out the dough onto a floured work surface and shape it. Cover the loaf with plastic wrap and let rise at room temperature for 2 to 4 hours or until about doubled.

Slash the top. Preheat the oven to 400 to 450° and bake for 40 to 45 minutes or until done. Cool on a wire rack.

Makes 1 loaf

Matthew's Semolina Bread II

(Refer to A Basic Sourdough Bread Loaf on page 26 for instructions and techniques.)

600 g. unbleached all-purpose flour

400 g. active starter

450 g. water

200 g. semolina flour

20 g. salt

In a large bowl, mix all the ingredients except the salt. Cover the dough with plastic wrap and let it sit at room temperature for about 30 minutes. Sprinkle the salt over the dough and mix well again to fully incorporate the salt throughout. Keeping the dough in the container, stretch and fold the dough every 30 minutes or so, about 5 or 6 times, covering the bowl with plastic wrap each time. Keeping the bowl covered, let the dough rise until about doubled, usually 4 to 8 hours or overnight.

Gently turn out the dough onto a floured work surface and shape it. Cover and let rise for 2 to 4 hours or until about doubled.

Slash the top. Preheat the oven to 400 to 450° and bake for 40 to 45 minutes or until done. Cool on a wire rack.

Makes 1 large or 2 small loaves

Matthew's White Bread

(Refer to A Basic Sourdough Bread Loaf on page 26 for instructions and techniques.)

800 g. unbleached all-purpose flour

400 g. active starter

400 g. water

20 g. salt

In a large bowl, mix all the ingredients except the salt. Cover the bowl and let the dough sit at room temperature for about 30 minutes. Sprinkle the salt over the dough and mix well again to fully incorporate the salt throughout. Keeping the dough in the container, stretch and fold the dough every 30 minutes or so, about 5 or 6 times, covering the bowl each time. Keeping the bowl covered, let the dough rise until about doubled, usually 4 to 8 hours or overnight.

Gently turn out the dough onto a floured work surface and shape it. Cover the loaf with plastic wrap and let rise for 2 to 4 hours or until about doubled.

Slash the top. Preheat the oven to 400 to 450° and bake for 40 to 45 minutes or until done. Cool on a wire rack.

Makes 1 large or 2 small loaves

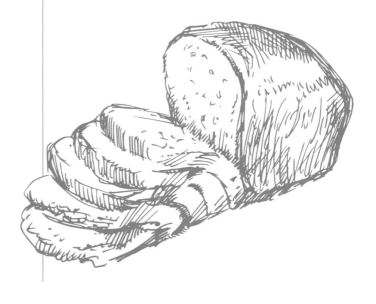

Oatmeal Bread

(Refer to A Basic Sourdough Bread Loaf on page 26 for instructions and techniques.)

3 cups all-purpose flour

2 cups active starter

1½ cups old-fashioned rolled oats

1 to 1½ cups milk, warmed to about 90°

3 T. honey

2 T. olive oil

1½ tsp. salt

In a large mixing bowl, combine all ingredients and mix until dough forms; cover the bowl and let the dough rest for 30 minutes.

Knead the dough for about 6 minutes, using flour to keep the dough from sticking but trying to use as little as possible so the dough remains soft (I usually do the kneading in the bowl). Turn out the dough into another large mixing bowl that has been greased. Cover and let the dough rise at room temperature for 2 hours.

Shape the dough and place it in a large, greased loaf pan. Cover and let rise at room temperature for another 2 to 4 hours.

Preheat the oven to 375° and bake for 50 to 55 minutes or until done. Remove the bread and let it cool on a wire rack for 15 to 20 minutes before slicing.

Makes 1 loaf

Roasted Garlic Bread

(Refer to A Basic Sourdough Bread Loaf on page 26 for instructions and techniques.)

800 g. unbleached all-purpose flour

20 g. salt

3 to 4 roasted garlic cloves, cut in half or thirds crosswise and then thinly sliced

400 g. active starter

400 g. water

In a medium mixing bowl, stir together the flour, salt, and roasted garlic pieces. Add the remaining ingredients, mix to combine, cover the bowl with plastic wrap, and then let the dough sit for about 30 minutes. Keeping the dough in the container, stretch and fold the dough every 30 minutes or so, about 6 times, covering the bowl with plastic wrap each time. Keeping the bowl covered, let the dough rise until about doubled, usually 4 to 8 hours or overnight.

Gently turn out the dough onto a floured work surface and shape it. Cover the loaf with plastic wrap and let rise for about 4 hours or until about doubled.

Slash the top. Preheat the oven to 400 to 450° and bake for 40 to 50 minutes or until done. Cool on a wire rack.

Makes 1 large or 2 small loaves

Rosemary Bread

(Refer to A Basic Sourdough Bread Loaf on page 26 for instructions and techniques.)

400 g. unbleached all-purpose flour

200 g. active starter

200 g. water

20 g. fresh rosemary, finely chopped or snipped

10 g. salt

In a large bowl, mix all the ingredients except the rosemary and salt. Cover the bowl with plastic wrap and let the dough sit at room temperature for about 30 minutes. Sprinkle the rosemary and salt throughout the dough and mix well again to fully incorporate the added ingredients. Keeping the dough in the container, stretch and fold the dough every 30 minutes or so, about 6 times, covering the bowl with plastic wrap each time. Keeping the bowl covered with plastic wrap, let the dough rise until almost doubled, usually between 4 to 8 hours or overnight.

Gently turn out the dough onto a floured work surface and shape it. Cover with plastic wrap and let rise for about 4 hours or until well risen.

Slash the top. Preheat the oven to 400 to 450° and bake for 40 to 50 minutes or until done. Cool on a wire rack.

Makes 1 loaf

Rye Bread

Prepare the starter 2 days before you plan to bake the bread.

Starter

240 g. water

240 g. unbleached all-purpose flour (or half all-purpose and half rye flour)

1 to 2 T. starter

Bread dough

Starter (made the previous evening)

1 cup milk

2 T. molasses

2 T. oil

2 tsp. salt

1 cup rye flour

5 cups unbleached all-purpose flour

1 egg, beaten

Caraway seed for sprinkling

Two days before baking:

In a large mixing bowl, combine the ingredients for the starter and mix well. Cover the bowl and let it rest on the counter overnight.

One day before baking:

In the large mixing bowl that holds the starter, add the milk, molasses, oil, and salt and mix until combined. Add the rye flour and mix again. Add the unbleached all-purpose flour, a bit at a time, and continue mixing. When the dough gets too stiff to mix by hand, turn it out onto a floured work surface and continue adding the flour by kneading in a bit at a time until the dough is smooth and satiny. Place the dough into a large mixing bowl, cover the bowl with plastic wrap, and place in the refrigerator until the early evening.

In the evening, take the bowl of dough, still covered by the plastic wrap, out of the refrigerator; let the dough sit on the counter overnight or 8 to 12 hours until the dough has about doubled in size.

Carefully turn out the risen dough onto a floured work surface, cover it, and allow it to rest for 30 minutes. Divide the dough into 2 equal pieces and shape it. Place the loaves on a baking sheet or in loaf pans, cover the loaves, and allow them to rise for 3 to 4 hours or until almost doubled in bulk.

Just before baking, brush the loaves with the beaten egg and sprinkle on the caraway seed. Slash the top of the loaves. Place the loaves in a cold oven, turn the oven to 375°, and bake for about 70 minutes or until done. Immediately after baking, remove the loaves to a wire rack to cool.

Makes 2 loaves

Soft Sandwich Bread

(Refer to A Basic Sourdough Bread Loaf on page 26 for instructions and techniques.)

28 g. butter

240 g. milk, heated almost to boiling

224 g. active starter

12 g. granulated sugar

9 g. salt

350 g. unbleached all-purpose flour

1 egg, beaten

Place the butter in the hot milk and stir to melt the butter; cool the milk mixture to 100°.

In a large mixing bowl, stir together the milk mixture, starter, sugar, and salt to combine. Add the flour a bit at a time until you can no longer mix the dough by hand. Turn out the dough onto a floured work surface and knead in the remaining flour. Continue kneading for several minutes, using as little extra flour as possible. The dough should be soft and slightly sticky.

Shape the dough into a round, smooth ball and place it in a large oiled or greased bowl, turning the dough to coat all surfaces. Cover the bowl with plastic wrap and allow it to rest at room temperature for 30 minutes.

Stretch and fold the dough a total of 2 times at 30-minute intervals and keeping the bowl covered between times. Let the covered dough rest at room temperature for 1 hour; then stretch and fold 3 times at 1-hour intervals, keeping the bowl covered between times.

By now, the dough should be very lively and light, but if not, cover the dough and let it rest for an hour or two longer.

Grease a loaf pan and set aside while you shape the dough to fit inside the loaf pan, being careful to gently form the dough to keep it light and airy. Place the dough into the prepared loaf pan, cover the pan with a damp kitchen towel or oiled plastic wrap (so the dough doesn't stick), and set it on the counter until the dough has risen to the top of the pan, or about doubled in bulk. (This should take between 1 and 2 hours.)

Preheat the oven to 350°. Slash down the middle of the loaf and bake it for 30 to 40 minutes or until the bread is done and the top is a light golden brown.

Let the bread sit in the loaf pan for 5 minutes before turning it out of the pan and placing it on a wire cooling rack until completely cool.

Makes 1 loaf

Spent-Grain Bread

(Refer to A Basic Sourdough Bread Loaf on page 26 for instructions and techniques.)

225 g. water

200 g. active starter

200 g. unbleached all-purpose flour

200 g. whole wheat flour

⅓ to ½ cup spent grain (see note)

10 g. salt

Note: Spent grain is what's left over from the beer brewing process. You can easily obtain spent grain by asking a friend who brews beer at home for their leftover spent grain, or you can call a local brewery—they will likely gladly give or sell you as much as you want. I get my spent grain from a local brewery, and once home, I measure the grain into ½-cup portions, remove as much air as I can, and freeze them in suitable containers. Thaw and use as needed.

In a large bowl, mix all ingredients except the spent grain and salt. Cover the bowl with plastic wrap and let the dough sit at room temperature for about 30 minutes. Sprinkle the spent grain and salt over the dough and mix well again to fully incorporate the salt throughout. Allow the dough to rest a second time, about 45 minutes. Keeping the dough in the container, stretch and fold the dough about 6 times at 30-minute intervals, covering the bowl with plastic wrap each time. Keeping the bowl covered with plastic wrap, let the dough rise until about doubled, usually 4 to 8 hours or overnight.

Gently turn out the dough onto a floured work surface and shape it. Cover with plastic wrap and let rise about 4 hours or until about doubled.

Slash the top. Preheat the oven to 400 to 450°and bake for 45 to 55 minutes or until done. Cool on a wire rack.

Makes 1 loaf

Sun-Dried Tomato and Basil Bread

(Refer to A Basic Sourdough Bread Loaf on page 26 for instructions and techniques.)

225 g. water

200 g. active starter

200 g. unbleached all-purpose flour

200 g. whole wheat flour

10 g. salt

30 g. sun-dried tomatoes, chopped into small pieces (no bigger than a chocolate chip)

1 heaping tsp. dried basil leaves (do not use ground basil)

In a large bowl, mix all the ingredients except the sun-dried tomatoes and basil. Let the dough sit for about 30 minutes. Keeping the dough in the container, stretch and fold the dough, cover the bowl, and let it rest for 30 minutes; stretch and fold the dough a second time, cover the bowl, and let it rest for another 30 minutes.

Now add the sun-dried tomatoes and basil, doing your best to sprinkle the pieces throughout the dough; stretch and fold the dough 4 more times, covering the bowl and letting the dough rest 30 minutes between each time. With each subsequent stretch and fold session, you'll notice that the sun-dried tomatoes and basil will become more evenly distributed throughout the dough.

Cover the bowl and let the dough rise until about doubled, usually 4 to 8 hours or overnight.

Gently turn out the dough onto a floured work surface and shape it. Cover and let rise for about 4 hours or until about doubled.

Slash the top. Preheat the oven to 400 to 450° and bake for 40 to 45 minutes or until done. Cool on a wire rack.

Makes 1 loaf

Sunflower Seed Bread

(Refer to A Basic Sourdough Bread Loaf on page 26 for instructions and techniques.)

240 g. active starter

1 T. butter

240 g. milk

½ cup raw sunflower seeds

1 T. honey

1 tsp. salt

175 g. whole wheat flour

140 g. durum flour (you can substitute half whole wheat and half unbleached all-purpose flour)

175 g. unbleached all-purpose flour

Pour the starter into a large mixing bowl and set aside for now.

The night before:

In a microwaveable bowl, melt the butter and then add the milk; stir in the sunflower seeds, honey, and salt. Check the temperature of the butter and milk mixture to make sure it's no warmer than 100°. When cool enough, add this mixture to the large mixing bowl that contains the starter and combine well. Add the whole wheat flour and durum and mix by hand. Start adding the all-purpose flour a bit at a time, mixing after each addition. When the dough becomes too stiff to mix by hand, turn out the dough onto a floured work surface and knead in the remaining flour. Continue kneading the dough until it's smooth and satiny (about 8 minutes). Cover the bowl with plastic wrap and let the dough sit at room temperature overnight to double in bulk.

The next morning:

Gently turn out the dough onto a floured work surface and allow the dough to rest for 30 minutes. Shape the dough into the shape you want. Place the loaf onto a baking sheet or into a loaf pan and let it rise at room temperature for 2 to 4 hours, or however long you need for the loaf to about double in size (if a loaf pan is used, let it rise to the top of the loaf pan).

Place the pan into a cool oven and then turn the oven to 375°. Bake for 65 to 70 minutes. Remove the bread from the oven (and loaf pan if using) and place it on a wire rack to cool.

Makes 1 loaf

Walnut Bread

(Refer to A Basic Sourdough Bread Loaf on page 26 for instructions and techniques.)

200 g. unbleached all-purpose flour

200 g. whole wheat flour

40 g. walnut pieces

10 g. salt

225 g. water

200 g. active starter

1 T. walnut oil (optional)

In a medium mixing bowl, stir together the flours, walnut pieces, and salt. Add the remaining ingredients, mix to combine, and then let the dough sit for about 30 minutes. Keeping the dough in the container, stretch and fold the dough every 30 minutes or so about 6 times. Cover the bowl and let the dough rise until about doubled, usually 4 to 8 hours or overnight.

Gently turn out the dough onto a floured work surface and shape it. Cover and let rise for about 4 hours or until about doubled.

Slash the top. Preheat the oven to 400 to 450° and bake for 40 to 50 minutes or until done. Cool on a wire rack.

Makes 1 loaf

Whole Wheat Bread

(Refer to A Basic Sourdough Bread Loaf on page 26 for instructions and techniques.)

400 g. whole wheat flour

250 g. water

200 g. starter

10 g. salt

In a large bowl, mix all the ingredients except the salt. Let the dough sit for about 45 minutes; sprinkle the salt over the dough and mix well again to fully incorporate the salt throughout. Keeping the dough in the container, stretch and fold the dough every 30 minutes or so about 6 times. Cover the bowl and let the dough rise until about doubled, usually 4 to 8 hours or overnight.

Gently turn out the dough onto a floured work surface and shape it. Cover and let rise for about 4 hours or until about doubled.

Slash the top. Preheat the oven to 400 to 450° and bake for 40 to 45 minutes or until done. Cool on a wire rack.

Makes 1 loaf

Whole Wheat Bread II

(Refer to A Basic Sourdough Bread Loaf on page 26 for instructions and techniques.)

800 g. whole wheat flour

500 g. water

400 g. starter

20 g. salt

In a large bowl, mix all the ingredients except the salt. Let the dough sit for about 30 minutes. Sprinkle the salt over the dough and mix well again to fully incorporate the salt throughout. Keeping the dough in the container, stretch and fold the dough every 30 minutes or so about 5 or 6 times. Cover the bowl and let the dough rise until about doubled, usually 4 to 8 hours or overnight.

Gently turn out the dough onto a floured work surface and shape it. Cover and let rise for 2 to 4 hours or until about doubled.

Slash the top. Preheat the oven to 400 to 450° and bake for 40 to 45 minutes or until done. Cool on a wire rack.

Makes 1 large or 2 small loaves

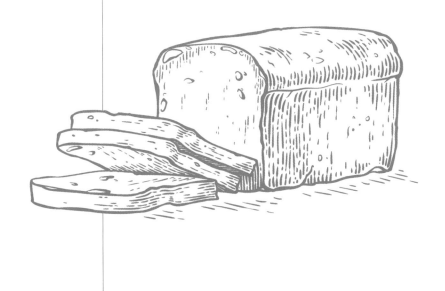

Chapter 8

BISCUITS, BAGELS, BUNS, ROLLS, AND MORE

This chapter is where the fun really begins, and it's a good introduction to the many uses for sourdough beyond a loaf of bread. Some of the recipes in this section need a long, slow rise the same as bread does, but there are plenty of recipes here that you can quickly make and bake.

Any of the bagel recipes are worth the hours needed to get them to the table, but be sure to try some of the quick and easy recipes, such as the Quick Buttermilk Biscuits or Beef and Vegetable Hand Pies. I think you'll be pleased.

Bacon and Cheese Biscuits

1 cup unbleached all-purpose flour

2 tsp. baking powder

½ tsp. baking soda

¼ tsp. salt

⅓ cup very cold butter, cubed

¾ cup shredded cheddar cheese

8 slices bacon, cooked, cooled, and crumbled

1 cup active starter

Preheat the oven to 425°. Line a baking sheet with a silicone baking mat or parchment paper; set aside for now.

In a medium mixing bowl, whisk together the flour, baking powder, baking soda, and salt. Using a pastry cutter or fork, mix in the butter until mixture has coarse crumbles, working quickly so the butter doesn't get too warm. Mix in the cheese and bacon. Next, add ¾ cup of the starter and mix until a soft dough forms, adding the remaining starter if needed.

Turn out the dough onto a floured work surface and gently knead a few times. Using your hands or a rolling pin, flatten the dough to about 1 inch thick. Using a floured biscuit cutter or a sharp knife, cut it into 10 to 12 biscuits. Place the biscuits on the prepared baking sheet and bake for 12 to 15 minutes or until puffed and golden.

Makes 10 to 12 biscuits

Bagels

2 cups active starter (480 g.)

2 eggs, beaten

½ cup milk

2 T. oil

4 T. granulated sugar, divided

1 tsp. salt

3 cups unbleached all-purpose flour

Note: I usually make a fresh batch of starter in the morning and then mix the dough that same evening so I can let it rise overnight and cook the bagels the next day.

Pour or scoop the starter into a large mixing bowl. Add the eggs, milk, oil, 2 tablespoons of sugar, and salt and combine. Add the flour, a bit at a time, and mix by hand. When the dough becomes too stiff to continue mixing by hand, turn out the dough onto a floured work surface and knead in the remaining flour until the dough is smooth and satiny (about 8 minutes). You can use additional flour if needed to keep the dough from sticking, but try to use as little extra flour as possible. The dough is very stiff, so you can use a stand mixer if you have one; knead with the dough hook for 5 to 7 minutes.

Place the dough into a clean container or large mixing bowl, cover with plastic wrap, and let it rise at room temperature for 8 to 12 hours or overnight.

Gently ease the dough out of the bowl onto a floured work surface. Divide the dough into 12 to 15 equal pieces. With your hands, make a ball and then roll the ball into a 6-inch-long rope. Bring the ends of the dough rope together to form a circle (like a donut) and pinch the ends together. Lay them out on the work surface or a piece of parchment paper. Cover with a kitchen towel and let the bagels rise at room temperature for 1 to 2 hours or until they are slightly puffed.

Preheat the oven to 425°.

Bring 4 quarts of water to a boil and add the remaining 2 tablespoons of sugar. Drop the bagels into the boiling water, being careful not to crowd them in the pot. When they rise to the surface, remove them with a slotted spoon, drain them on a kitchen towel (or you can use paper towels), and then place them on a baking sheet that has been lined with greased parchment paper or a silicone baking mat.

Turn down the oven to 375° and place the bagels in the oven to bake for 25 to 30 minutes or until they are a deep golden brown. Place them on a wire rack to cool.

Makes 12 to 15 bagels

Beef and Vegetable Hand Pies

Crust

226 g. very cold butter (2 sticks) or cold shortening

250 g. unbleached all-purpose flour

6 g. salt

3 g. granulated sugar

250 g. discard starter (discard straight from the refrigerator works best)

10 g. white vinegar

Filling

½ lb. ground beef

2 T. unbleached all-purpose flour

1 T. fresh parsley, minced, or 1 tsp. dried parsley flakes

¾ tsp. salt

1 tsp. beef bouillon granules, or 1 beef bouillon cube

¼ cup hot water

¾ cup potatoes, peeled and diced small

Using the larger holes on a box grater, shred the butter into a large mixing bowl. Work quickly so the butter remains as cold as possible.

In another bowl, whisk together the flour, salt, and sugar; add these ingredients to the mixing bowl and toss the ingredients to coat and separate the butter shreds. Continue with a pastry cutter to cut the butter into the flour mixture until it forms large crumbs.

Add the discard starter and vinegar and use a fork to combine them with the flour mixture. When the dough begins to hold together, use your hands to quickly work the dough so there are no more dry bits of flour. If the dough seems too dry, you can add a teaspoon or two of very cold water (ice water if you have it).

Cut the dough into 6 equal portions; wrap each portion with plastic wrap and refrigerate the dough while you make the meat filling.

Brown the ground beef in a skillet just until the meat is no longer pink; drain the grease. Add the flour, parsley, and salt and stir well to coat the meat with the flour. Dissolve the bouillon in the hot water and stir into the meat mixture. Continuing to stir, add the potatoes, carrots, and onion. Cover and cook over medium heat until the vegetables are crisp tender. Take the skillet off the heat and allow the mixture to cool.

Preheat the oven to 400°. Line a baking sheet with parchment paper or a silicone baking mat.

Remove the pastry from the refrigerator and roll out each

½ cup carrots, peeled and diced small

2 T. onion, finely chopped

1 egg, beaten together with 2 T. water and a pinch of salt (for the egg wash)

piece to an 8-inch circle. Place about ⅓ heaping cup of the meat mixture slightly off-center on each circle of dough. Moisten the edge of the dough and fold the dough over to form a half-circle. Crimp the edges together with a fork to seal the edges. With a very sharp knife, cut a 1-inch-long slit in the top. Brush the tops of the hand pies with the egg wash.

Place the hand pies on the prepared baking sheet and turn down the heat to 350°. Immediately place the baking sheet in the oven and bake the pies for 35 to 40 minutes or until the tops are browned.

Makes 6 pies

Blueberry Bagels

2 cups active starter (480 g.)

2 eggs, beaten

½ cup milk

½ cup blueberries, fresh, dried, frozen and thawed, or canned and drained

2 T. oil

4 T. granulated sugar, divided

1 tsp. salt

3 cups unbleached all-purpose flour

Note: I usually make a fresh batch of starter in the morning and then mix the dough that same evening so I can let the dough rise overnight and cook the bagels the next day.

Pour or scoop the starter into a large mixing bowl. Add the eggs, milk, blueberries, oil, 2 tablespoons of sugar, and salt and stir to combine. Add the flour, a bit at a time, and mix by hand. When the dough becomes too stiff to continue mixing by hand, turn out the dough onto a floured work surface and knead in the remaining flour until the dough is smooth and satiny (about 7 minutes). You can use additional flour if needed to keep the dough from sticking, but try to use as little extra flour as possible. The dough is very stiff, so you can use a stand mixer if you have one; knead with the dough hook for 5 minutes.

Place the dough into a clean container or large mixing bowl, cover with plastic wrap, and let it rise at room temperature for 8 to 12 hours or overnight.

Gently ease the dough out of the bowl onto a floured work surface. Divide the dough into 12 to 15 equal pieces. With your hands, make a ball and then roll the ball into a 6-inch-long rope. Bring the ends of the dough rope together to form a circle (like a donut) and pinch the ends together. Lay them out on the work surface or a piece of parchment paper. Cover with a kitchen towel and let the bagels rise at room temperature for 1 to 2 hours or until they are slightly puffed.

Preheat the oven to 425°.

Bring 4 quarts of water to a boil and add the remaining 2 tablespoons of sugar. Drop the bagels into the boiling water, being careful not to crowd them in the pot. When they rise to the surface, remove them with a slotted spoon, drain them on a kitchen towel (or you can use paper towels), and then place them on a baking sheet that has been lined with greased parchment paper or a silicone baking mat.

Turn down the oven to 375° and place the bagels in the oven to bake for 25 to 30 minutes or until they are a deep golden brown. Place them on a wire rack to cool.

Makes 12 to 15 bagels

Butterhorns

1 cup milk

½ cup water

½ cup (1 stick) butter, plus a bit more for brushing

½ cup granulated sugar

2 tsp. salt

4½ cups unbleached all-purpose flour, divided

1 cup starter

3 eggs

In a medium saucepan, stir together the milk, water, ½ cup butter, sugar, and salt and heat on low until the butter has melted. Place the mixture into a large mixing bowl and cool to barely warm. Add 2 cups of the flour and combine. Add the starter and mix again. Cover the bowl with plastic wrap and let it sit at room temperature for about 8 hours or overnight.

Add enough of the remaining flour to make a soft, loose dough that is somewhat sticky. Add the eggs one at a time, mixing well after each addition. Cover the bowl and let it sit at room temperature for 2 hours.

Turn out the dough onto a floured work surface and cut it into 3 equal portions. Roll out each portion into a thick circle somewhat thicker than a pie crust. Brush each circle with melted butter and then cut each circle into 12 wedges as though you're cutting a pie. Roll up each wedge, starting at the fat end and rolling toward the point. Place the rolls on baking sheets that are lined with a silicone baking mat or parchment paper. Cover the rolls and let them sit at room temperature until light and fluffy (about 2 hours).

Preheat the oven to 350°. Bake for 15 minutes or until the rolls are a light golden brown and cooked through.

Serve plain or with powdered sugar sprinkled on top.

Makes 36

Cheddar Cheese Bagels

2 cups active starter (480 g.)

2 eggs, beaten

½ cup milk

½ cup sharp cheddar cheese, shredded, plus a bit more for sprinkling on top

2 T. oil

3 T. granulated sugar, divided

1 tsp. salt

3 cups unbleached all-purpose flour

Note: I usually make a fresh batch of starter in the morning and then mix the dough that same evening so I can let the dough rise overnight and cook the bagels the next day.

Pour or scoop the starter into a large mixing bowl. Add the eggs, milk, cheddar cheese, oil, 1 tablespoon of sugar, and salt and stir to combine. Add the flour, a bit at a time, and mix by hand. When the dough becomes too stiff to continue mixing by hand, turn out the dough onto a floured work surface and knead in the remaining flour until the dough is smooth and satiny (about 8 minutes). You can use additional flour if needed to keep the dough from sticking, but try to use as little extra flour as possible. The dough is very stiff, so you can use a stand mixer if you have one; knead with the dough hook for 5 to 7 minutes.

Place the dough into a clean container or large mixing bowl, cover with plastic wrap, and let it rise at room temperature for 8 to 12 hours or overnight.

Gently ease the dough out of the bowl onto a floured work surface. Divide the dough into 12 to 15 equal pieces. With your hands, make a ball and then roll the ball into a 6-inch-long rope. Bring the ends of the dough rope together to form a circle (like a donut) and pinch the ends together. Lay them out on the work surface or a piece of parchment paper. Cover with a kitchen towel and let the bagels rise at room temperature for 1 to 2 hours or until they are slightly puffed.

continued...

Preheat the oven to 425°.

Bring 4 quarts of water to a boil and add the remaining 2 tablespoons of sugar. Drop the bagels into the boiling water, being careful not to crowd them in the pot. When they rise to the surface in about 30 seconds (or a bit longer), remove them with a slotted spoon, drain them on a kitchen towel (or you can use paper towels), and then place them on a baking sheet that has been lined with greased parchment paper or a silicone baking mat. Sprinkle the tops of the bagels with a small amount of shredded cheese if desired.

Turn down the oven to 375° and place the bagels in the oven to bake for 25 to 30 minutes or until they are a deep golden brown. Place them on a wire rack to cool.

Makes 12 to 15 bagels

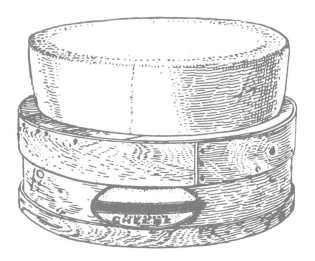

Cheese and Chive Biscuits

1 cup unbleached all-purpose flour

2 tsp. baking powder

½ tsp. baking soda

¼ tsp. salt

¾ cup shredded sharp cheddar cheese

½ cup snipped chives

⅓ cup very cold butter, cubed

1 cup active starter

Preheat the oven to 425°. Line a baking sheet with a silicone baking mat or parchment paper; set aside for now.

In a medium mixing bowl, whisk together the flour, baking powder, baking soda, and salt. Add the cheese and chives. Using a pastry cutter or fork, mix in the butter until mixture has coarse crumbles, working quickly so the butter doesn't get too warm. Next, add ¾ cup of the starter and mix until a soft dough forms, adding the remaining starter if needed.

Turn out the dough onto a floured work surface and gently knead it a few times. Using your hands or a rolling pin, flatten the dough to about 1 inch thick. Using a floured biscuit cutter or a sharp knife, cut it into 10 to 12 biscuits. Place the biscuits on the prepared baking sheet and bake for 14 to 16 minutes or until puffed and golden.

Makes 10 to 12 biscuits

Cheese and Jalapeño Bagels

2 cups active starter
(480 g.)

2 eggs, beaten

½ cup milk

⅓ cup sharp cheddar
cheese, shredded,
plus a bit more for
sprinkling on top

2 T. oil

3 T. granulated sugar,
divided

1 tsp. salt

¼ cup finely chopped
pickled, roasted,
or fresh jalapeño
peppers

3 cups unbleached
all-purpose flour

Note: I usually make a fresh batch of starter in the morning and then mix the dough that same evening so I can let the dough rise overnight and cook the bagels the next day.

Pour or scoop the starter into a large mixing bowl. Add the eggs, milk, cheese, oil, 1 tablespoon of sugar, salt, and peppers and stir to combine. Add the flour, a bit at a time, and mix by hand. When the dough becomes too stiff to continue mixing by hand, turn out the dough onto a floured work surface and knead in the remaining flour until the dough is smooth and satiny (about 8 minutes). You can use additional flour if needed to keep the dough from sticking, but try to use as little extra flour as possible. The dough is very stiff, so you can use a stand mixer if you have one; knead with the dough hook for 5 to 7 minutes.

Place the dough into a clean container or large mixing bowl, cover with plastic wrap, and let it rise at room temperature for 8 to 12 hours or overnight.

Gently ease the dough out of the bowl onto a floured work surface. Divide the dough into 12 to 15 equal pieces. With your hands, make a ball and then roll the ball into a 6-inch-long rope. Bring the ends of the dough rope together to form a circle (like a donut) and pinch the ends together. Lay them out on the work surface or a piece of parchment paper that has been lightly dusted with flour. Cover with a kitchen towel and let the bagels rise at room temperature for 1 to 2 hours or until they are slightly puffed.

Preheat the oven to 425°.

Bring 4 quarts of water to a boil and add the remaining 2 tablespoons of sugar. Drop the bagels into the boiling water, being careful not to crowd them in the pot. When they rise to the surface in 30 seconds or so, remove them with a slotted spoon, drain them on a kitchen towel (or you can use paper towels), and then place them on a baking sheet that has been lined with greased parchment paper or a silicone baking mat. Sprinkle the tops of the bagels with a small amount of shredded cheese if desired.

Turn down the oven to 375° and place the bagels in the oven to bake for 25 to 30 minutes or until they are a deep golden brown. Place them on a wire rack to cool.

Makes 12 to 15 bagels

Cinnamon Raisin Bagels

2 cups active starter (480 g.)

2 eggs, beaten

½ cup milk

½ cup raisins

2 T. oil

4 T. granulated sugar, divided

1 tsp. salt

1 tsp. ground cinnamon

3 cups unbleached all-purpose flour

Note: I usually make a fresh batch of starter in the morning and then mix the dough that same evening so I can let the dough rise overnight and cook the bagels the next day.

Pour or scoop the starter into a large mixing bowl. Add the eggs, milk, raisins, oil, 2 tablespoons of sugar, salt, and cinnamon and stir to mix. Add the flour, a bit at a time, and mix by hand. When the dough becomes too stiff to continue mixing by hand, turn out the dough onto a floured work surface and knead in the remaining flour until the dough is smooth and satiny (about 8 minutes). You can use additional flour if needed to keep the dough from sticking, but try to use as little extra flour as possible. The dough is very stiff, so you can use a stand mixer if you have one; knead with the dough hook for 5 to 7 minutes.

Place the dough into a clean container or large mixing bowl, cover with plastic wrap, and let it rise at room temperature for 8 to 12 hours or overnight.

Gently ease the dough out of the bowl onto a floured work surface. Divide the dough into 12 to 15 equal pieces. With your hands, make a ball and then roll the ball into a 6-inch-long rope. Bring the ends of the dough rope together to form a circle (like a donut) and pinch the ends together.

Lay them out on the work surface or a piece of parchment paper. Cover with a kitchen towel and let the bagels rise at room temperature for 1 to 2 hours or until they are slightly puffed.

Preheat the oven to 425°.

Bring 4 quarts of water to a boil and add the remaining 2 tablespoons of sugar. Drop the bagels into the boiling water, being careful not to crowd them in the pot. When they rise to the surface, remove them with a slotted spoon, drain them on a kitchen towel (or you can use paper towels), and then place them on a baking sheet that has been lined with greased parchment paper or a silicone baking mat.

Turn down the oven to 375° and place the bagels in the oven to bake for 25 to 30 minutes or until they are a deep golden brown. Place them on a wire rack to cool.

Makes 12 to 15 bagels

Cornbread

1 cup starter (discard is fine)

1 cup buttermilk

1 cup cornmeal

1 cup unbleached all-purpose flour

2 eggs

½ cup butter, melted and cooled but still liquid

¼ cup sugar

½ tsp. salt

2 tsp. baking powder

½ tsp. baking soda

In a medium mixing bowl, mix the starter, buttermilk, cornmeal, and flour. (You can cover the bowl with plastic wrap and set it aside at room temperature for an hour or two to further develop flavor or continue immediately with the next steps.)

Preheat the oven to 350°. Generously grease or butter a 9-inch cast-iron skillet, deep dish pie plate, or baking dish and set aside while you finish mixing the batter.

To the flour mixture, add the eggs, butter, sugar, and salt and stir to combine. Add the baking powder and baking soda and stir again.

Place the batter into the prepared baking container and smooth the top of the batter. Bake for 35 to 40 minutes or until light brown on top and the middle is cooked through. Allow the cornbread to cool for about 10 minutes before slicing.

Serves 6 to 8

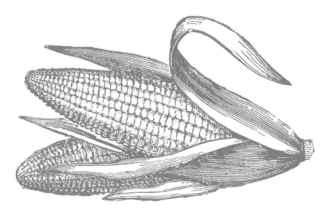

Dinner Rolls

(Refer to A Basic Sourdough Bread Loaf on page 26 for instructions and techniques.)

Starter

60 g. unbleached all-purpose flour

60 g. water

24 g. starter

12 g. granulated or caster sugar

Dinner rolls

75 g. butter

Starter made the evening before

440 g. unbleached all-purpose flour

180 g. water, room temperature or slightly tepid

115 g. milk

23 g. granulated or caster sugar

10 g. salt

1 egg, beaten with 1 T. milk for egg wash

The night before:

In a wide-mouth quart canning jar or medium-sized mixing bowl, mix the starter ingredients. Cover with plastic wrap and leave it at room temperature overnight.

The next morning:

Cut the butter into ½-inch pieces; set the pieces in a small bowl and set aside for a half hour or so to come to room temperature.

In the bowl of a stand mixer, place the starter along with the softened butter and all the other roll ingredients except the egg-and-milk wash. Turn to low speed and mix until there are no more dry bits of flour present. Turn the mixer to medium speed and continue to mix until dough forms and begins to pull away from the sides (3 to 5 minutes). Turn out the dough into a large bowl and cover the bowl with plastic wrap. Rest the dough for 30 minutes and then perform 3 stretch and fold sessions 30 minutes apart, covering the bowl between sessions. Keeping the bowl covered, let the dough rise at room temperature for 2½ more hours.

Before shaping, refrigerate the dough for 20 minutes—this will make it easier to shape the rolls because the dough is very soft and airy.

Prepare a 9 x 9-inch baking dish by generously buttering the inside or place a piece of parchment paper cut to fit inside the pan.

Carefully turn out the dough onto a floured work surface.

continued...

Using a bench scraper or sharp knife, divide the dough into 16 equal portions. Shape each piece of dough into a tight ball. Place the balls of dough into the baking dish in 4 rows across and 4 rows down.

Cover the baking dish with plastic wrap and let the rolls rise at room temperature for about 3 hours. The dough should have risen to about the top of the baking dish and be very soft. If it isn't, let the dough continue to rise and check again every half hour.

Preheat the oven to 425°.

Make the egg wash and beat the mixture very well until frothy. Brush the tops of the rolls with the egg wash and place the baking dish on the middle rack in the oven. Bake for 20 minutes and then turn down the oven to 375° and continue baking for 15 to 20 minutes or until the tops are golden brown.

Remove from the oven and let the rolls sit in the baking dish for 5 minutes before removing them to a wire rack to cool further.

Makes 16 rolls

English Muffins

½ cup starter discard

2¾ cups unbleached all-purpose flour, divided

1 cup milk

1 T. granulated sugar

1 tsp. baking soda

¾ tsp. salt

Cornmeal for dusting

In a large mixing bowl, stir together the starter and 2 cups of the flour. Cover with plastic wrap and set it out at room temperature for 8 to 10 hours or overnight.

Add the remaining flour, milk, sugar, baking soda, and salt and combine well. Turn out the dough onto a floured work surface and knead it until it is smooth and elastic (4 to 5 minutes).

Roll out or pat the dough to ½ inch thick and cut the English muffins with a 3-inch biscuit or cookie cutter. Before rerolling the scraps to cut more muffins, let the dough rest for 10 minutes.

Sprinkle cornmeal on a baking sheet or piece of parchment and place the muffins on the sheet. Let the muffins sit at room temperature for at least 1 hour.

Lightly grease a griddle or skillet (cast iron works the best). Heat to medium-low and then cook the English muffins for about 6 minutes per side or until they are cooked through and golden brown on top. Be careful to keep the heat low enough so the muffins cook through without becoming burnt. Set the muffins on a wire rack or paper towels to cool completely. Instead of cutting the English muffins with a knife, use a fork to poke holes all around the edges and then tear them apart.

Makes 12 muffins

Everything Bagels

Ingredients for Everything Spice Seasoning:

2 T. poppy seeds

1 T. plus 1 tsp. dried minced onion

1 T. plus 1 tsp. dried minced garlic

1 T. white sesame seeds

1 T. black sesame seeds

2 tsp. coarse salt or coarse sea salt

1 batch of plain bagels, ready to parboil and bake (see recipe for Bagels on page 66)

To make the Everything Spice Seasoning, mix all the ingredients except the bagels in a small container with a tight-fitting lid.

As soon as the bagels are taken out of the boiling water, set them on a silicone baking mat or greased parchment paper and sprinkle liberally with the Everything Spice Seasoning. (The seed and spices will adhere to the bagel while they are still wet.) Bake according to the Bagels recipe directions.

Makes 12 to 15 bagels

German Rye and Wheat Rolls

(Refer to A Basic Sourdough Bread Loaf on page 26 for instructions and techniques.)

Sourdough starter

150 g. rye flour

150 g. water

1 T. starter

Yeast starter

150 g. whole wheat flour

150 g. water

1.5 g. yeast (instant or active dry)

German Rye and Wheat Rolls

Sourdough starter

Yeast starter

450 g. whole wheat flour

250 g. rye flour

18 g. salt

3 g. yeast (instant or active dry)

1 tsp. barley malt syrup (can substitute an equal amount of molasses or honey)

The night before:

In a wide-mouth quart canning jar or small mixing bowl, mix the sourdough starter ingredients, stirring until well combined. Cover the top with plastic wrap and let it sit at room temperature for about 12 hours or overnight.

In a separate wide-mouth quart canning jar or small mixing bowl, mix the yeast starter ingredients, stirring until well combined. Cover the top with plastic wrap and let it sit at room temperature for about 12 hours or overnight.

The next morning:

In a large mixing bowl, combine all the ingredients. Mix by hand until no bits of dry flour remain (or as close as you can get). Cover the bowl with plastic wrap and let the dough sit at room temperature for 30 minutes to help hydrate the flours.

Stretch and fold the dough at 30-minute intervals, covering the dough between each session, at least 6 times or until the dough is smooth and light.

Cut the dough into 18 equal portions and shape the pieces into batards (they look like torpedoes). Place the rolls on baking sheets that have been lined with a silicone baking mat or parchment paper. Cover the rolls with a kitchen towel and let them rest at room temperature for 45 to 60 minutes.

Preheat the oven to 400°. Right before baking, slash the tops of each roll lengthwise down the middle. Bake for 15 to 20 minutes or until lightly browned. Remove from the oven and set the rolls on a wire rack to cool. *Makes 18 rolls*

Hamburger Buns

(Refer to A Basic Sourdough Bread Loaf on page 26 for instructions and techniques.)

430 g. unbleached all-purpose flour, divided

240 g. milk, slightly warm

60 g. active starter

2 eggs, divided

2 T. granulated sugar

1 tsp. active dry yeast

1 tsp. salt

3 T. butter, softened to room temperature

2 tsp. sesame seeds (optional)

In a stand mixer with a dough hook, combine 300 grams of the flour with the milk, starter, 1 of the eggs, and the sugar, yeast, and salt. Beat on low to medium speed until a shaggy dough forms. Cover the mixture with a damp cloth or plastic wrap and let the dough rest for 30 minutes.

Still using the dough hook, knead the dough for 7 to 8 minutes, gradually adding the remainder of the flour interspersed with pieces of the butter. The dough should be soft and sticky but able to pull away from the sides of the bowl.

Using a spatula or dough scraper, turn out the dough into a large, greased mixing bowl. Cover the bowl with plastic wrap and let it rest at room temperature for 2 to 3 hours or until the dough is about doubled in bulk.

Turn out the dough onto a floured work surface and divide it into 8 equal portions. Shape the dough into tight balls as you would shape a round loaf. Place the shaped buns an inch or more apart onto a baking sheet that has been lined with a silicone baking mat or parchment paper. Cover the buns with a damp kitchen towel and let them rise at room temperature for 1½ to 2 hours or until they have about doubled in bulk and the sides are touching.

Preheat the oven to 375°.

Beat the second egg together with 2 tablespoons of water, and brush the tops of the buns with the egg wash. Sprinkle the buns with the sesame seeds if using. Bake the buns for 20 to 22 minutes or until golden brown. Remove the buns from the oven and place them on a wire rack to cool for about 20 minutes before slicing. *Makes 8 buns*

Hot Dog Buns

1 cup milk, warmed to 100°

3 T. granulated sugar

½ cup active starter, or ½ cup discard plus 1 tsp. instant yeast

400 g. bread flour or unbleached all-purpose flour

2 T. butter, room temperature, plus 2 T. melted butter for brushing tops of buns

1 tsp. salt

In the bowl of a stand mixer equipped with a dough hook, stir together the milk and sugar until the sugar is dissolved. Add the starter (and the yeast, if using) and stir to mix. Add the flour and mix on low speed until the dough forms. Add the room temperature butter in small pieces and then the salt; knead the dough on medium speed for about 5 minutes or until the dough is smooth.

Transfer the dough to a large, greased mixing bowl and cover the bowl with plastic wrap. Let the dough rise until about doubled in bulk at room temperature—about 3 hours if you have used yeast or 8 to 10 hours if you have used starter only.

Turn out the dough onto a floured work surface and divide it into 8 equal portions. Cover with plastic wrap and let it rest for 20 to 30 minutes.

Shape each piece into a smooth log about 6 inches long. Place the buns on a baking sheet that has been lined with a silicone baking mat or parchment paper at least an inch apart. Cover the buns with greased plastic wrap or a damp kitchen towel and let them rise for 1 to 2 hours or until about doubled in bulk.

Preheat the oven to 350°. Bake the hot dog buns for 28 to 30 minutes or until golden brown. Remove from the oven and immediately brush the buns with the melted butter. Allow the buns to cool completely before slicing.

Makes 8 buns

Overnight Biscuits

Starter

240 g. water

240 g. flour

1 to 2 T. starter

Biscuits

140 g. (1 cup) un-bleached all-purpose flour

1 T. granulated sugar

1 tsp. baking soda

½ tsp. salt

120 g. (½ cup) cold butter, cut into small cubes

Starter that you made earlier

The night before:

In a medium mixing bowl, stir together all the starter ingredients. Cover and let the mixture sit on the counter overnight for morning biscuits or until about doubled and bubbly if baking the same day (4 to 6 hours).

The next morning:

In a large mixing bowl, whisk together the flour, sugar, baking soda, and salt. Using a fork or a pastry blender, cut in the butter until the mixture resembles coarse crumbs. Add the starter and stir with a fork. Add a little flour or milk if needed so the dough is soft and moist and barely pulls away from the sides of the bowl. Turn out the dough onto a floured work surface and knead it for several minutes, adding flour as necessary to keep stickiness to a minimum.

With a floured rolling pin, roll out the dough to about ½ inch thick. Cut it into 2-inch biscuits using a floured biscuit cutter or a sharp knife. Place the biscuits on a baking sheet, either spread out for crisper sides or with sides touching for softer biscuits. Cover the biscuits and let them rise for about 2 hours.

Preheat your oven to 375°. Bake the biscuits for 20 to 25 minutes or until a light golden color.

Makes about 8 biscuits

Pizza Crust

(Refer to A Basic Sourdough Bread Loaf on page 26 for instructions and techniques.)

240 g. starter

240 g. water

3 T. olive oil

360 g. flour (all-purpose is fine, but bread flour makes a chewier crust)

2 tsp. salt

Start 1 or 2 days before you plan to have pizza.

In a medium mixing bowl, stir together the starter, water, and olive oil. Add the flour and salt and stir well; the dough will be soft and feel sticky. Cover the bowl with plastic wrap and let the dough rest for 30 minutes.

Stretch and fold the dough at half-hour intervals a total of 4 times, covering the bowl after each time. Cover the dough and let it rest at room temperature for 4 hours.

Turn out the dough onto a floured work surface and divide it into 3 equal amounts. Shape the dough into balls and then set them inside 3 well-oiled storage containers a pint or so in size. Cover the containers (lids are fine in this instance, or use plastic wrap held down with rubber bands) and refrigerate the dough overnight. You can refrigerate the dough for about 5 days before using, or freeze the dough, wrapped tightly in several layers of plastic wrap, for up to a month.

When ready to bake, remove the dough from the refrigerator and turn it out onto a floured work surface. Cover the dough with a towel and let it rest for 30 minutes. With your hands, gently flatten and stretch the dough into a thin circle about 10 inches in diameter. If the dough springs back excessively, cover it and let it rest for another 15 minutes and then try again. Add your desired toppings on the crust.

Preheat the oven to 450 to 500°. Bake the pizza for 8 to 10 minutes or until done.

Makes 3 pizza crusts

Pretzels

1½ cups starter (discard is fine to use)

1 cup milk, slightly warm

2 T. butter, soft

1 T. granulated sugar

4 cups unbleached all-purpose flour

1 T. baking soda

1 egg beaten with 1 T. water for brushing tops

2 tsp. coarse salt for sprinkling

In the bowl of a stand mixer that has a dough attachment, combine the starter, milk, butter, and sugar on the lowest speed. Add the flour and mix on low speed for 5 minutes.

Grease a large mixing bowl and scrape out the dough from the stand mixer into the mixing bowl. Cover with plastic wrap and let sit at room temperature for 2 hours.

Turn out the dough onto a floured work surface and gently knead it for about 3 minutes. Cut or tear the dough into 12 equal pieces. Roll each piece of dough into a long rope about 1 inch thick. Form each piece into the shape of a pretzel and then place the pretzels on baking sheets that have been lined with a silicone baking mat or parchment paper; freeze for 25 minutes.

Preheat the oven to 450°.

While the pretzels are in the freezer, fill a large pot with water and stir in the baking soda to dissolve it. Heat the water to a strong boil. Remove the pretzels from the freezer and place them into the boiling water, being careful not to crowd them, and boil for 30 seconds. Remove the pretzels with a slotted spoon and place them back onto the prepared baking sheets. Brush the pretzels with the egg wash and sprinkle them with the coarse salt.

Bake for 15 to 18 minutes or until a light golden brown. Set the pretzels on a wire rack to cool.

Makes 12 pretzels

Quick Biscuits

1 cup unbleached all-purpose flour or bread flour

2 tsp. baking powder

½ tsp. salt

½ tsp. baking soda

6 T. very cold butter, cut into small cubes

1 cup starter (discard is fine)

Preheat the oven to 425°.

In a medium mixing bowl, whisk together the flour, baking powder, salt, and baking soda. Cut the butter into the flour mixture using a fork or pastry cutter until the mixture looks like coarse crumbs. Add the starter and mix with a spoon until the flour is mostly combined. Knead the dough in the bowl with your hands for a minute or so until the dough comes together.

Turn out the dough onto a floured work surface and then roll or pat it to ¾ inch thick. Cut the biscuits with a floured biscuit cutter or sharp knife. Gather the scraps together, roll them out again, and cut more biscuits to get as many as possible. (I usually end up with a smaller, misshapen biscuit at the end, but it tastes just as good as the pretty ones!)

Place the biscuits on an ungreased baking sheet, either spread out for crisper sides or with the sides touching for softer biscuits.

Bake for 12 to 15 minutes or until done. (If the biscuits are touching, it may take a few more minutes for them to fully bake.)

Makes about 8 biscuits

Quick Buttermilk Biscuits

2 cups unbleached all-purpose flour

2 tsp. granulated sugar

2 tsp. baking powder

1 tsp. salt

¾ tsp. baking soda

½ cup (1 stick) very cold butter

1 cup active starter

½ cup buttermilk

Preheat the oven to 425°. Line a baking sheet with a silicone baking mat or parchment paper and set it aside for now.

In a large mixing bowl, whisk together the flour, sugar, baking powder, salt, and baking soda. Cut the butter into very small pieces or shred using the large holes of a box grater. Add to the flour mixture and stir to mix the butter pieces throughout.

In a medium mixing bowl, stir together the starter and buttermilk. Add the starter mixture to the flour mixture and stir (a rubber spatula works well because you can clean the sides of the bowl as you work) until a soft dough begins to form. Turn out the dough onto a lightly floured work surface and knead it several times until it comes together.

Roll out or pat the dough to about 1½ inches thick. Cut it into 8 to 10 biscuits, using a 2-inch biscuit cutter or a sharp knife. Place the biscuits onto an ungreased baking sheet, either spread out for crisper sides or with sides touching for softer biscuits.

Bake for 12 to 15 minutes or until done. (If the biscuits are touching, it may take a few more minutes for them to fully bake.)

Makes 8 to 10 biscuits

Rustic Flatbread

2 cups unbleached all-purpose flour

1 tsp. salt

1 tsp. baking powder

1 cup starter discard

½ cup milk

1 T. olive oil, plus more for cooking and for brushing the flatbread

Toppings of your choice (optional)

In a large mixing bowl, whisk together the flour, salt, and baking powder. Add the starter, milk, and 1 tablespoon olive oil, and stir with a large spoon until dough begins to form. (I use my hands after a bit of stirring with the spoon.)

Turn out the dough onto a floured work surface and gently knead or stretch and fold for several minutes, adding flour as needed, until the dough is smooth and no longer sticky. Wrap the ball of dough with plastic wrap and let it sit at room temperature for 30 minutes.

Preheat a cast-iron skillet to medium-high heat.

Cut the dough into 6 equal portions and roll out each piece to about ¼ inch thick. Lightly brush one side of the flatbread with olive oil and place it on the heated skillet, oiled side down. Fry the flatbread for about 1½ minutes; brush the top side of the flatbread with oil and then flip it over to fry the second side for about 1 minute. Fry all the pieces in the same way, stacking the flatbreads on a plate covered with a doubled kitchen towel to keep warm.

These flatbreads taste great plain, but when you flip them to cook the second side, you can sprinkle on any toppings you desire. Some good options include coarse salt, minced garlic and/or onion, finely shredded hard cheese, and fresh snipped or dried herbs.

Makes 6

Sage Croutons

6 slices sourdough bread, cubed

4 T. olive oil

4 T. butter, melted

4 T. minced fresh sage

Place the bread cubes in a small bowl; drizzle with oil, melted butter, and sage. Toss them to coat.

Cook the bread cubes on the stovetop over medium heat until golden brown, stirring them to cook all sides (6 to 8 minutes).

Amounts vary depending on the size of slices, but I usually get about 6 cups.

Slow-Rise Rye Bagels

Starter

1 cup unbleached all-purpose or bread flour

1 cup water

½ cup active starter

½ cup rye flour

Bagels

2 cups rye flour

1 T. barley malt syrup, or you can substitute an equal amount of honey, molasses, or brown sugar

2 tsp. caraway seeds

1 tsp. salt

1 T. baking soda (for parboil on second day)

1 T. brown sugar (for parboil on second day)

The night before:

In the evening, combine all the starter ingredients in a large mixing bowl, cover the bowl with plastic wrap, and set it on the counter overnight.

The next morning:

In the bowl containing the active starter, add all the bagel ingredients and mix as well as you can. Cover the bowl and let the dough rest for 30 minutes (it will be shaggy and not very cohesive). After the rest period, turn out the dough onto a floured work surface and knead it for 10 minutes—you can knead in the traditional way or do continual stretch and folds for the allotted time. Add more rye flour if needed while kneading. (This will be hard work!)

Cover the dough loosely with plastic wrap, leaving plenty of room for the dough to expand, and let it sit at room temperature for 8 to 12 hours or until about doubled.

Turn out the dough onto a lightly floured work surface and cut it into 16 equal portions. Cover the portions and let them rest at room temperature for 30 minutes so the dough relaxes a bit. Using your hands, roll each piece of dough into a 6-inch-long rope and then form the dough into a circle, pinching the ends together to make a donut shape. Lay out the bagels at least one inch apart on a large baking sheet lined with a silicone baking sheet or piece of greased parchment paper. Cover them with plastic wrap and let them rise at room temperature for 1 hour. Refrigerate the bagels, still covered, overnight.

continued...

In the morning, take the bagels out of the refrigerator and let them rest at room temperature for at least an hour or until they are room temperature.

Preheat the oven to 425°. Prepare a large baking sheet (you may have to use 2 baking sheets) by lining with a silicone baking mat or parchment paper.

Fill a large pot with water and add 1 tablespoon each of baking soda and brown sugar; mix until dissolved. Bring the water to a strong boil.

Add the bagels to the boiling water, being careful not to crowd them. Boil for 20 seconds, flip them over, and boil the second side for about 15 seconds. Remove them with a slotted spoon and set them on a clean kitchen towel. When all the bagels have been parboiled, place them back on the baking sheet and bake them for 20 to 30 minutes or until they are golden brown on top and done. Place them on a wire rack to cool.

Makes 12 bagels

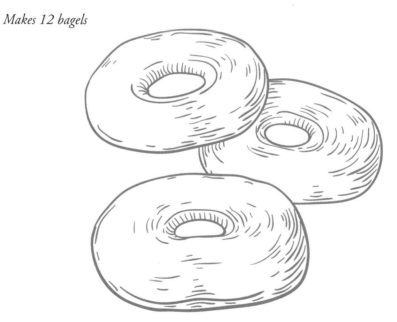

Wheat Bagels

2½ to 3 cups un-bleached all-purpose flour

1 cup active starter

1 cup whole wheat flour

1 cup water

3 T. brown sugar, divided

2 tsp. salt

1½ tsp. instant yeast

1 egg, beaten together with 2 T. water for brushing on the bagels

In a large mixing bowl, mix 2½ cups of the all-purpose flour with the starter, whole wheat flour, water, 2 tablespoons of the brown sugar, and the salt and yeast. Turn out the dough onto a floured work surface and knead it for about 5 minutes, adding the remaining flour as needed but using as little as possible.

Place the dough in a large, greased bowl and cover the bowl with plastic wrap. Let the dough rise at room temperature for 30 minutes.

Turn out the dough onto a lightly floured work surface and cut it into 12 equal portions. Using your hands, roll each piece of dough into a 6-inch-long rope and then form the dough into a circle, pinching the ends together to make a donut shape. Lay out the bagels on a silicone baking sheet or piece of greased parchment paper. Cover the bagels with plastic wrap and let them rise at room temperature for 1 hour.

Preheat the oven to 425°. Line a large baking sheet with a silicone baking mat or parchment paper. Set aside for now.

Fill a large pot with water and stir in the remaining tablespoon of brown sugar; bring the water to a strong boil.

Drop the bagels, a few at a time, into the boiling water, being careful not to crowd them. Boil them for about 20 seconds and then turn them over (use a slotted spoon) to boil the second side for another 15 to 20 seconds. Remove the bagels and set them on the prepared baking sheet. Brush the tops of the bagels with the egg wash and bake them for 25 minutes or until browned on top. Place on a wire rack to cool.

Makes 12 bagels

Wheat Pizza Crust

1½ cups active starter

¾ cup whole wheat flour

¾ cup unbleached all-purpose or bread flour

2 T. vegetable oil

1 T. honey

1 tsp. salt

1 heaping tsp. dried oregano leaves

1 heaping tsp. dried basil leaves

¼ tsp. garlic powder

¼ tsp. onion powder

¼ cup water, more or less

In a large mixing bowl, mix the starter, flours, oil, honey, salt, herbs, and spices. Add the water, a small amount at a time and mixing as you go, adding just enough water so no dry bits of flour remain. Knead the ball of dough for a minute or two, cover the bowl with plastic wrap or a damp kitchen towel, and let it sit at room temperature for 2 to 3 hours.

Preheat the oven to 450°. Cut a piece of parchment paper that is slightly larger than the pizza or baking stone or cast-iron skillet you plan to use for baking the crust and set aside for now. Place a baking sheet on the bottom rack of the oven and then place a pizza stone or cast-iron skillet onto the middle rack of the oven to preheat.

Lightly flour the parchment paper. Lightly flour the dough and then roll out or pat the dough to fit the parchment paper. Poke some holes in the dough with a fork and then let the dough rest at room temperature for 15 minutes.

Transfer the crust (still on the parchment paper) onto the preheated pizza stone or skillet and bake for 8 minutes. Remove from the oven and add toppings of your choice. Put the pizza back in the oven and bake for another 12 to 15 minutes or until done.

Makes 1 large pizza crust

Chapter 9

BREAKFAST GOODIES

I'm a firm believer in a breakfast of substance. It wakes up our bodies and brains and helps to keep us going for hours. The recipes in this section give us a lot to choose from, and they are super tasty—one more reason not to skip this all-important meal.

Learning to make pancakes is a must-have skill in my opinion, and you can find several delicious options in this section. Apple Fritters and Dutch Babies are always a hit, especially with the youngsters, and who wouldn't be charmed to be eating Toad in the Hole?

Apple Fritters

3 cups diced apples, peeled or left with skins on

1 cup starter (discard is fine)

½ tsp. ground cinnamon

¼ tsp. salt

¼ tsp. baking soda

Oil for frying

Cinnamon sugar for sprinkling (optional)

Place the diced apples in a large mixing bowl. Slowly add the starter, mixing gently as you go, until combined. (You want the apple pieces well coated with starter, so you might need to add a bit more starter to achieve that—it helps to keep the fritters together when you fry them.)

Whisk together the cinnamon, salt, and baking soda and gently stir the mixture into the apples. Let the mixture rest while you heat the oil for frying.

Put about 2 inches of oil in a heavy cast-iron deep-sided skillet and heat to 360 to 370°. Drop the fritter batter into the hot oil, being careful not to crowd them. Fry for 2 to 3 minutes on each side or until golden brown. Use a slotted spoon to place the fritters on paper towels to drain. Sprinkle with cinnamon sugar if using and serve.

Makes about 20 small fritters or 12 large fritters

Apple Fritters on the Fly

Leftover starter (¼ cup for small batch up to 1 cup or more for a family)

2 to 4 apples, seeded, peeled, and diced

¼ to ½ tsp. cinnamon

⅛ to ¼ tsp. baking soda

⅛ tsp. salt

2 to 4 T. granulated sugar (optional)

Note: No need to throw away your leftover starter after you've refreshed a new batch. Instead, give this recipe a try. You can "eyeball" the amounts because nothing can go wrong with this easy recipe.

Mix all the ingredients until well blended, adding the sugar to taste if you prefer sweeter fritters. Heat about ½ inch of oil in a cast-iron pan (if you have one) or other suitable pan. Use oil that has a high smoke point, such as avocado oil or ghee (although I often use lard or vegetable oil and have no problems if I carefully watch my pan). Drop a tablespoon or two of batter per fritter into the hot oil and cook on one side for about 3 minutes; turn and cook the other side for 2 to 3 minutes or until done. Blot the fritters on paper towels and eat them plain or with maple syrup, cinnamon sugar, or powdered sugar on top. Or make a glaze with powdered sugar and milk, adding the milk in small quantities and then stirring until you have a consistency you're pleased with.

Amounts vary depending on how much leftover starter you have

Apple Pancakes

180 g. milk

120 g. unbleached all-purpose flour

225 g. starter

14 g. butter, melted and slightly cooled

14 g. baking powder

13 g. granulated sugar (use a bit more if your apple is tart)

6 g. salt

5 g. ground cinnamon

1 apple, peeled, cored, cut into eighths, and thinly sliced crosswise

In a medium mixing bowl, combine the milk and flour; let sit at room temperature for 20 minutes.

Add the remaining ingredients and stir well. Fold in the apple slices.

Pour ¼ cup of batter per pancake into a heated and greased pan or skillet and cook for about 3 minutes; flip the pancakes and cook the second side until done (about 2 minutes).

Number of pancakes varies depending on size of individual pancakes

Bacon Breakfast Casserole

4 to 5 cups sourdough bread, cut into 1-inch cubes

8 eggs

1¼ cups milk

1 cup shredded cheddar cheese

½ tsp. salt

½ tsp. pepper

2 T. chopped green onions (optional)

12 slices bacon, cooked and crumbled

The night before:

Butter or grease a 9 x 13-inch baking dish. Evenly layer the bread cubes across the bottom.

In a large mixing bowl, beat the eggs; add the milk, cheese, salt, pepper, and green onions (if using) and mix. Add the bacon and mix again until well combined. Pour the egg mixture over the bread cubes in the baking dish and gently stir and press the mixture so the eggs penetrate to the bottom of the baking dish and all the ingredients are fully incorporated. Cover the casserole with aluminum foil and refrigerate it overnight. (If you make it the same morning you plan to eat it, let the casserole sit at room temperature for about 45 minutes before baking.)

The next morning:

Preheat the oven to 350°. Bake the casserole for 30 minutes and then remove the aluminum foil and continue baking for 25 to 35 more minutes or until a knife inserted in the middle comes out clean. Cool for 5 minutes before serving.

Serves 8

Blueberry Pancakes

1½ cups starter (discard is fine)

1 cup milk (room temperature if you have the time)

2 eggs (room temperature if you have the time)

¼ cup butter, melted and cooled slightly

1 tsp. vanilla extract

1½ cups unbleached all-purpose flour

1 tsp. baking soda

1 tsp. baking powder

½ tsp. salt

1 pt. blueberries (you can use fresh, canned and drained, or frozen berries that have been thawed and drained)

In a large mixing bowl, whisk together the starter, milk, eggs, butter, and vanilla extract. Mix in the dry ingredients one at a time until well blended. Gently fold in the blueberries.

Pour ¼ cup batter per pancake into a heated and greased pan or skillet and cook for about 3 minutes; flip the pancakes and cook the second side until done (about 2 minutes).

Number of pancakes varies depending on size of individual pancakes, but this recipe makes plenty for a family

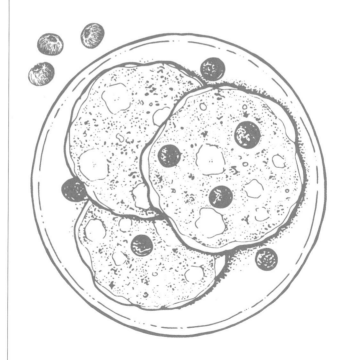

Blueberry Waffles

2 cups active starter

1 cup fresh blueberries

2 eggs, yolks separated

2 T. butter, melted and cooled slightly

2 tsp. granulated sugar

1 tsp. salt

½ to 1 cup unbleached all-purpose flour

½ tsp. baking soda dissolved in 1 T. water

In a medium bowl, mix the starter, blueberries, egg yolks, butter, sugar, and salt until well combined. Add the flour a bit at a time until a thick but pourable consistency is attained and the batter is lump-free.

Beat the egg whites until soft peaks form and then gently fold into the batter.

Just before cooking, gently stir in the dissolved baking soda.

Cook the waffles according to your waffle iron's directions. Top the waffles with butter and syrup or powdered sugar.

Makes 4 to 6 waffles

Brunch Casserole

Butter for spreading

6 slices sourdough bread, more or less (you'll need 4 to 5 cups)

1 lb. bulk pork sausage, cooked just enough to get the pink out and then drained

2 cups cheddar cheese, shredded

½ red bell pepper, cut into small pieces

¼ cup chopped green onions

3 eggs, beaten

1 can condensed cream of asparagus soup

2 cups milk

¼ cup chicken broth or white wine

½ tsp. Dijon mustard

¼ tsp. ground black pepper

The night before:

Butter the bread and cut it into cubes; place into a greased or buttered 9 x 13-inch baking dish. Sprinkle the bread with the sausage, cheese, bell peppers, and green onions.

In a medium mixing bowl, stir together the eggs, soup, milk, broth or wine, mustard, and pepper. Pour over the bread mixture. Cover the baking dish with plastic wrap and refrigerate overnight.

The next day:

Remove the casserole from the refrigerator 30 minutes before baking. Preheat the oven to 350°. Uncover and bake the casserole for 45 to 55 minutes or until a knife inserted in the middle comes out clean.

Let stand 5 minutes before cutting.

Serves 8

Buckwheat Pancakes

1 cup unbleached all-purpose flour

1 cup buckwheat flour

2 T. granulated sugar

2 tsp. baking powder

1 tsp. baking soda

½ tsp. salt

1½ cups milk

1 cup recently fed starter

1 egg, beaten

2 T. oil

In a large mixing bowl, whisk together the flours, sugar, baking powder, baking soda, and salt. Add the milk, starter, egg, and oil and mix gently to combine. If the batter seems too thick, you can add a small amount of milk or water to thin it.

Pour no more than ¼ cup batter per pancake into a heated and greased pan or skillet and cook for about 3 minutes; flip the pancakes and cook the second side until done (about 2 minutes).

Serve with butter, syrup, or jam.

Number of pancakes varies depending on size of individual pancakes, but this recipe makes plenty for a family

Buttermilk Pancakes

2 cups all-purpose flour

2 T. granulated sugar

1½ tsp. baking powder

½ tsp. baking soda

½ tsp. salt

1⅓ cups buttermilk

1 cup recently fed starter

1 egg, beaten

2 T. vegetable oil

In a mixing bowl, whisk together the flour, sugar, baking powder, baking soda, and salt. Add the remaining ingredients and gently mix together.

Pour ¼ cup batter per pancake into a heated and greased pan or skillet and cook for about 3 minutes; flip the pancakes and cook the second side until done (about 2 minutes).

Number of pancakes varies depending on size of individual pancakes, but this recipe makes plenty for a family

Cinnamon Rolls

(Refer to A Basic Sourdough Bread Loaf on page 26 for instructions and techniques.)

Dough

160 g. milk

115 g. butter, melted

1 egg

100 g. active starter

24 g. granulated sugar

360 g. unbleached all-purpose flour

5 g. salt

Cinnamon filling

2 T. butter

½ cup granulated sugar

1 T. flour

3 tsp. ground cinnamon

Glaze

2 T. butter, softened to room temperature

½ cup whipped cream cheese, room temperature

½ cup powdered sugar

1 to 2 T. milk as needed

The night before:

In a small mixing bowl, whisk together the milk and butter; let the mixture cool until slightly tepid. Using a stand mixer and regular beaters, combine the egg, starter, and granulated sugar; mix to blend well. With the mixer running, slowly add the milk mixture, blending the entire time. Add the flour and salt a bit at a time, continuing to mix for about 2 minutes, scraping down the sides as you mix. Cover the bowl with a damp kitchen towel and let the dough rest for 30 minutes.

Attach the dough hook to the mixer and knead the dough on medium-low speed for 6 to 8 minutes. If the dough is very sticky and doesn't pull away from the sides, add a bit more flour.

Butter or grease a medium mixing bowl and transfer the dough to the bowl. Cover the bowl with plastic wrap and let the dough rest at room temperature for 30 minutes. Perform 2 stretch and fold sessions 30 minutes apart, covering the bowl between each session. Cover the bowl with plastic wrap and let the dough rise overnight at room temperature.

The next morning:

Line a 9-inch cake pan with parchment paper and lightly spray the paper. Set aside for now.

Grease and then flour your work surface; make the prepared area large enough to roll out the dough to a 12 x 16-inch rectangle. Gently turn out the dough into the middle of the prepared work surface. Let the dough rest for about 15 minutes to relax the dough. This resting period will make it possible to roll the dough out. To roll the dough into a 12 x 16-inch rectangle, first flour the surface of the dough as well as the rolling pin. If the dough resists being rolled out and bounces back, let it rest for another 5 minutes or so and then roll out again.

Once the dough is rolled out, make the **cinnamon filling** by melting the butter and letting it cool slightly. While the melted butter is cooling, in another small bowl mix the remaining cinnamon filling ingredients.

Brush the melted butter on the surface of the dough; sprinkle the surface of the dough with the cinnamon sugar mixture, leaving ½ inch around the edges free of the cinnamon sugar.

Roll the dough into a tight log (you may need to flour or oil your hands if the dough is very sticky) going from one 16-inch side to the other 16-inch side. When done rolling the log, make sure the seam side is down (on the work surface). Cut the log into 8 pieces, about 2 inches thick, and transfer them to the prepared cake pan. Cover with a kitchen towel and let them rise until slightly puffy, about 2 hours.

Preheat the oven to 350°.

Bake the cinnamon rolls for 30 to 40 minutes or until the tops are a light golden brown. Let the cinnamon rolls rest in the pan for 15 minutes before removing them, still on the parchment paper, to a wire rack to continue cooling. While the cinnamon rolls are cooling, mix the **glaze** ingredients; use an electric mixer for a smoother glaze and add milk a bit at a time until you have the desired consistency for spreading. When the cinnamon rolls are cool, spread the glaze across the tops.

Makes 8 rolls

Dutch Baby

Starter

160 g. water

160 g. flour

1 to 2 T. starter

Dutch baby

6 T. butter

320 g. starter (made
the night before)

6 eggs, beaten

⅓ cup milk

½ tsp. salt

The night before:

In a large mixing bowl, combine all ingredients for the starter. Cover and set the bowl on the counter to rise overnight.

The next morning:

Preheat the oven to 425°. Place the butter in a large cast-iron deep-sided skillet or Dutch oven. Place the pan in the oven to melt the butter, watching it so the butter melts but doesn't scorch.

While the butter is melting and the oven is preheating, in the large bowl that contains the starter, add the eggs, milk, and salt. Mix until the batter is very smooth.

Using oven mitts, remove the pan from the oven and tilt the pan so the inside is coated. Pour the batter into the pan and return it to the oven. Bake for 15 to 20 minutes or until the Dutch baby is golden brown on top and has puffed up the sides of the pan.

Cut the Dutch baby as you would a pie. Serve the slices plain or with a bit of butter, powdered sugar, maple syrup, or fresh berries.

Serves 4 to 6

Hot Cereal

2 cups starter

1½ cups water

¼ tsp. salt

In a medium saucepan, mix the starter, water, and salt. Bring to a simmer, stirring occasionally so the bottom doesn't scorch. Lower the temperature to low heat and continue to cook for another few minutes or until it has thickened slightly. Serve with some milk, a pat of butter, and sugar to taste.

Makes about 4 servings

Light and Airy Waffles

2 cups active starter

2 eggs, yolks separated

¼ cup milk

2 T. butter, melted and cooled slightly

1 T. granulated sugar

1 tsp. salt

½ to 1 cup unbleached all-purpose flour

In a medium mixing bowl, stir together the starter, egg yolks, milk, butter, sugar, and salt. Add enough flour, a bit at a time, to attain a pourable but thick batter and mix well so the batter no longer has any lumps. Cover the bowl and let it sit at room temperature for 1½ hours.

Beat the egg whites until soft peaks form and then gently fold them into the batter.

Cook the waffles according to your waffle iron's directions. Top the waffles with butter, syrup, jam, or fruit and sweetened whipped cream.

Makes about 6 waffles

Oatmeal Pancakes

1 cup starter (discard is fine)

1 cup rolled oats (old-fashioned un-cooked oatmeal)

1 cup milk

1 egg, beaten

2 T. butter, melted, plus more butter or oil for cooking

2 T. granulated sugar

1 tsp. baking powder

1 tsp. baking soda

½ tsp. salt

In a large mixing bowl, combine the starter, rolled oats, and milk; cover and let it rest on the counter for 30 minutes.

Gently whisk in the egg, melted butter, sugar, baking powder, baking soda, and salt.

Pour ¼ cup batter per pancake into a heated and greased pan or skillet (cast iron works well) and cook for about 3 minutes; flip the pancakes and cook the second side until done (about 2 minutes). Serve plain or with butter, maple syrup, or jam.

Number of pancakes varies depending on size of individual pancakes

Overnight Pancakes

Starter

1½ cups unbleached all-purpose flour

1 cup milk

½ cup starter (discard is fine to use)

Batter

2 eggs

2 T. butter, melted and then cooled slightly

2 T. granulated sugar

1 tsp. baking powder

½ tsp. salt

The night before:

In a large bowl, mix the flour, milk, and starter; cover and let sit on the counter overnight.

The next morning:

In a separate bowl, mix the eggs, butter, sugar, baking powder, and salt. Spoon this mixture into the starter mixture and gently stir to combine. Cover the bowl and let it rest for about 15 minutes.

Pour ¼ cup batter per pancake into a heated and greased pan or skillet and cook for about 3 minutes; flip the pancakes and cook the second side until done (about 2 minutes).

Number of pancakes varies depending on size of individual pancakes

Pumpkin Pancakes

2 eggs, yolks separated

300 g. buttermilk

150 g. active starter

80 g. pumpkin puree (plain)

180 g. unbleached all-purpose flour

2 T. granulated sugar

1 tsp. salt

1 tsp. baking soda

1 tsp. baking powder

½ to ¾ tsp. ground cinnamon

⅛ tsp. ground nutmeg (optional)

¼ cup butter (½ stick), melted

Separate the eggs: Place the whites in a medium-sized mixing bowl and set aside for now; place the yolks in another medium-sized mixing bowl. Whisk the yolks to break; add the buttermilk, starter, and pumpkin puree and whisk again to combine the ingredients.

In a large mixing bowl, whisk together the flour, sugar, salt, baking soda, baking powder, cinnamon, and nutmeg (if using). Add the starter mixture and stir. Next, add the melted butter and stir again but just enough that no dry bits of flour remain.

Whisk or use a handheld mixer to beat the egg whites until stiff peaks form and then fold them into the batter.

Pour ¼ cup batter per pancake into a heated and greased pan or skillet and cook for about 3 minutes; flip the pancakes and cook the second side until done (about 2 minutes).

Number of pancakes varies depending on size of individual pancakes

Quick Pancakes

2 cups unbleached all-purpose flour

2 T. granulated sugar

2 tsp. baking powder

1 tsp. baking soda

½ tsp. salt

1½ cups milk

1 cup recently fed starter

1 egg, beaten

2 T. oil

Whisk together the flour, sugar, baking powder, baking soda, and salt. Add the milk, starter, egg, and oil and gently combine.

Pour ¼ cup batter per pancake into a heated and greased pan or skillet and cook for about 3 minutes; flip the pancakes and cook the second side until done (about 2 minutes).

Serve with butter, syrup, or jam.

Makes 12 to 16 pancakes

Quick Waffles

1 cup starter or discard

⅔ cup milk

2 T. oil

1 T. granulated sugar

2 eggs

1 cup unbleached all-purpose flour

1 tsp. baking soda

Preheat your waffle iron.

In a medium mixing bowl, add the starter, milk, oil, sugar, and eggs; mix well.

Whisk together the flour and baking soda and stir it into the starter mixture. If needed, add a bit more milk or flour to get the right batter consistency.

Following the directions that came with your waffle iron, pour the batter into your waffle iron and cook. Serve immediately, topped with butter, syrup, jam, etc.

Amounts vary depending on the size waffle iron you use, but I get 5 waffles per batch

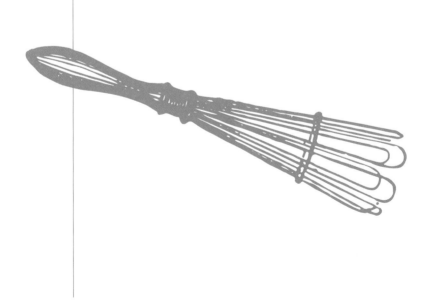

Rye Pancakes

480 g. active starter

1 egg, beaten

120 g. milk

30 g. butter, melted and cooled slightly

25 g. granulated sugar

6 g. salt

115 g. rye flour

Unbleached all-purpose flour as needed

½ tsp. baking soda dissolved in 1 T. water

In a medium mixing bowl, stir together the starter, egg, milk, butter, sugar, and salt until well combined. Add the rye flour and stir again; add enough all-purpose flour to attain the desired pancake batter consistency. Mix thoroughly so there are no lumps in the batter. Right before ready to begin cooking, pour in the dissolved baking soda and mix thoroughly again.

Pour ¼ cup batter per pancake into a heated and greased pan or skillet and cook for about 3 minutes; flip the pancakes and cook the second side until done (about 2 minutes).

Serve with butter, syrup, jam, or sweetened applesauce.

Makes 10 to 12 pancakes

Sausage and Sourdough Bread Strata

4 cups sourdough bread, cubed

1 lb. breakfast sausage or Italian sausage, cooked and crumbled

2 cups sharp cheddar cheese, shredded (if you buy a block of cheese and shred it yourself, the cheese is meltier)

12 eggs

2¼ cups milk

2 tsp. dry ground mustard

1 tsp. salt

½ tsp. ground pepper

Assemble the strata the night before so you can bake it in the morning. This recipe uses sourdough bread and is great for using up leftover bread.

The night before:

Grease or butter a 9 x 13-inch baking dish. Mix the bread cubes and cooked sausage and spread evenly across the bottom of the pan. Next, sprinkle the shredded cheese evenly over the top of the sausage and bread.

In a medium mixing bowl, beat together the eggs, milk, dry mustard, salt, and pepper until thoroughly combined. Pour the egg mixture over the bread cubes, sausage, and cheese. Cover the baking dish with aluminum foil, crimping the edges for a snug fit. Refrigerate overnight.

The next day:

Remove the strata from the refrigerator, leave it covered, and set it on the counter to warm up a bit (about 30 minutes).

Preheat the oven to 350°. Bake the strata for 30 minutes, still covered with the aluminum foil; remove the foil and continue baking for 25 to 30 more minutes or until the strata is puffed and the middle is set. Cut it into squares and serve.

Makes 8 to 12 squares

Sourdough Bread French Toast

This recipe is great for using up leftover sourdough bread that is going stale.

4 eggs

½ cup milk

Salt and pepper to taste

8 thick slices sourdough bread

Butter for cooking

In a flat-bottomed dish such as a glass pie plate or baking dish, beat together the eggs, milk, and salt and pepper until well mixed. (You can also use a blender to mix the ingredients.) Add the slices of sourdough bread and let them soak up the egg mixture.

Melt some butter in a skillet or griddle over medium heat; add the soaked slices of bread and cook for several minutes or until the bottom is golden brown; flip the French toast and cook the second side until done and golden brown. Be careful to watch the temperature so the French toast doesn't burn or get too dark before cooked through.

Serve plain or with butter, powdered sugar, or maple syrup.

Makes 8 slices

Toad in the Hole

Butter for spreading, room temperature

6 slices thick-sliced sourdough bread with a hole cut or torn out of the middle, about 4 inches in diameter (or use a biscuit cutter)

6 eggs

Salt and pepper to taste

Spread butter on both sides of the bread slices.

Set the bread on a preheated skillet. Cook on medium-low heat until the undersides are golden brown and toasted. Turn the bread over and crack an egg into the hole of each piece of bread. Sprinkle with salt and pepper if desired (or salt and pepper them at the table when serving). Cover the skillet and cook until the egg whites are set. If desired, you can quickly flip the pieces of toast over to the first side to cook the eggs a bit firmer.

Serves 6

Whole Wheat Pancakes

2½ cups whole wheat flour (whole wheat pastry flour will make a somewhat lighter and fluffier pancake, but it's not necessary)

2 cups milk

1 cup starter

2 T. oil

2 eggs

¼ cup sugar

2 tsp. baking soda

1 tsp. salt

In a large mixing bowl, combine the flour, milk, starter, and oil until blended but not smooth. Let it sit at room temperature for 30 minutes.

Add the eggs, sugar, baking soda, and salt and mix again. If a few lumps remain, that's fine.

Pour ¼ cup batter per pancake into a heated and greased pan or skillet and cook for about 3 minutes; flip the pancakes and cook the second side until done (about 2 minutes).

Number of pancakes varies depending on size of individual pancakes

Chapter 10

MUFFINS, SWEETS, AND SPECIALTIES

This section has the most varied selection of recipes, and if your family is like mine, they'll love everything here. The Coffee Cake recipe is quick and easy and is always a hit, and the Mix-in-the-Pan Chocolate Cake recipe is a simple classic. If savory is more your style, whip up a batch of Tortillas and fill them with some Fried Fish. But no matter which recipe you choose, you're sure to have a winner on your hands.

Amish Friendship Bread

Bread dough

2 cups unbleached all-purpose flour

1 cup Amish Friendship Bread starter (see Amish Friendship Bread starter recipe on page 132)

1 cup oil

1 cup granulated sugar

2 small boxes instant vanilla pudding (3.4 ounces each)

3 eggs

½ cup milk

2 tsp. ground cinnamon

1½ tsp. baking powder

½ tsp. salt

½ tsp. baking soda

½ tsp. vanilla extract

1 cup chopped walnuts or pecans (optional)

Dusting loaf pans

½ cup granulated sugar

1½ tsp. ground cinnamon

Preheat the oven to 325°.

In a large mixing bowl, add all the ingredients for the bread and mix well.

In a separate small bowl, mix the ingredients for dusting the loaf pans.

Grease 2 loaf pans. Dust the prepared pans with half of the cinnamon and sugar mixture. Pour in the batter evenly between both loaf pans and sprinkle the remaining cinnamon and sugar mixture on top of the batter.

Bake for 1 hour or until a toothpick inserted into the center of the loaf comes out clean. Cool the bread in the loaf pans until they loosen from the pans and then place them on a platter to continue cooling.

Makes 2 loaves

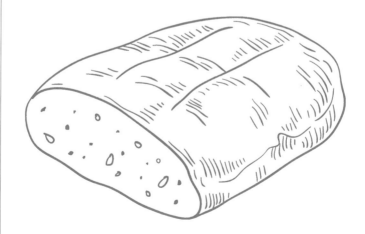

Amish Friendship Bread Starter

Starter

¼ cup water, 110°

1 pkg. (2¼ tsp.) active dry or instant yeast

1 cup unbleached all-purpose flour

1 cup granulated sugar

1 cup milk

You may be wondering why I'm including this recipe in a book on sourdough. Amish Friendship Bread *is* a sourdough recipe. It's a sweet sourdough base, and while there are recipes that have been developed expressly for this starter, you can experiment with making the sweet recipes in this book as well. Amish Friendship Bread has been around for years, and even though folks often have a love/hate relationship with it, I thought including it here would be fun.

Day 1. Pour the warm water into a small glass mixing bowl; sprinkle the yeast over the water and let it rest for 5 to 8 minutes so the yeast fully dissolves.

In a larger glass mixing bowl, whisk together the flour and sugar. Using a wooden or stainless-steel spoon, stir in the milk. Next add the yeast mixture and stir again. Cover the bowl with plastic wrap and allow it to stand until bubbly. This won't take long because of the yeast.

Once the mixture is bubbly, pour it into a gallon-sized freezer bag that has a zippered closure. Seal the bag, working to get all the air out before closing completely. Let the bag sit at room temperature throughout the entire process that follows.

Days 2, 3, 4, and 5. Do not open the bag; mash the bag to mix the ingredients.

Day 6. Add 1 cup each of unbleached all-purpose flour, granulated sugar, and milk. Mash the bag until the ingredients are mixed well; close the bag, being careful to get out all the air.

Days 7, 8, and 9. Do not open the bag; mash the bag to mix the ingredients.

Day 10. Pour the starter batter into a large glass mixing bowl and add ½ cup each of unbleached all-purpose flour, granulated sugar, and milk. Mix well with a wooden or stainless-steel spoon.

Divide the starter batter into 1-cup portions, placing them in separate 1-gallon freezer bags that have a zippered closure; mash each bag to remove the air and then close it. You'll get 4 to 5 bags' worth.

Give away bags to friends and keep one for yourself. Or keep two for yourself—one to make a fresh batch of starter and one to use for baking the Amish Friendship Bread recipe. Use a permanent marker to write the daily instructions on the bags you give away, or print out the instructions.

This is considered **Day 1** for the fresh batch.

Amish Friendship Chocolate Chip Bread

Bread dough

1 cup Amish Friend-ship Bread starter (see Amish Friendship Bread Starter recipe on page 132)

3 eggs

1 cup oil

½ cup milk

½ tsp. vanilla extract

2 small boxes instant chocolate pudding (3.4 ounces each)

2 cups unbleached all-purpose flour

1 cup granulated sugar

½ cup cocoa powder

1½ tsp. baking powder

½ tsp. salt

½ tsp. baking soda

1 cup chocolate chips, tossed with 1 to 2 tablespoons flour to help them "float" while baking

Dusting

½ cup granulated sugar

½ tsp. cocoa powder

Preheat the oven to 325°.

In a large mixing bowl, add the starter, eggs, oil, milk, and vanilla extract; mix well.

In another bowl, whisk together the chocolate pudding mixes, flour, sugar, cocoa powder, baking powder, salt, and baking soda. Add the flour mixture to the starter mixture and stir well to blend. Add the prepared chocolate chips and gently mix to combine.

In a small bowl, mix the sugar and cocoa powder for dusting.

Grease 2 loaf pans. Dust the prepared pans with half of the cocoa and sugar mixture. Pour in the batter evenly between both loaf pans and sprinkle the remaining cocoa and sugar mixture on top of the batter.

Bake for 1 hour or until a toothpick inserted into the center of the loaf comes out clean. Cool the bread in the loaf pans until they loosen from the pans and then place them on a platter to continue cooling.

Makes 2 loaves

Applesauce Muffins

¾ cup starter

½ cup applesauce

⅓ cup rolled oats

¼ cup molasses

¼ cup granulated sugar

1 egg

1⅓ cups unbleached all-purpose flour, divided

1½ tsp. baking powder

1 tsp. ground cinnamon

½ tsp. salt

Preheat the oven to 375°. Grease a muffin tin or use paper liners that have been lightly sprayed with oil.

In a large mixing bowl, stir together the starter, applesauce, rolled oats, molasses, sugar, and egg. Add 1 cup of the flour along with the baking powder, cinnamon, and salt and stir well. Add a bit more of the flour if the batter seems too thin. The batter should be thick enough that you have to spoon it into the muffin cups.

Fill the muffin cups two-thirds full and bake them for 20 to 25 minutes. Cool for a few minutes in the muffin tin and then remove the muffins and place them on a wire rack to cool further.

Makes 12 muffins

Banana Bread

2 cups unbleached all-purpose flour

½ tsp. baking soda

½ tsp. salt

½ cup (1 stick) butter, softened to room temperature

½ cup brown sugar

½ cup granulated sugar

2 eggs

1 cup mashed bananas (3 to 4 bananas)

1 tsp. vanilla extract

1 cup starter

Preheat the oven to 350°. Grease or spray a loaf pan and set aside for now.

In a medium mixing bowl, whisk together the flour, baking soda, and salt.

In a large mixing bowl, combine the butter with both sugars. Use an electric mixer to beat the ingredients until smooth. Add the eggs, bananas, and vanilla; mix until well blended.

Add the flour mixture and starter to the wet mixture and stir by hand.

Pour the batter into the prepared loaf pan and bake for 55 to 65 minutes or until a toothpick inserted into the center comes out with crumbs but not wet batter.

Cool in the pan.

Makes 1 loaf

Banana Bread Pudding

Bread pudding

4 cups cubed sour-dough bread, cut into 1-inch pieces (day-old works best)

¼ cup butter, melted

3 eggs

2 cups milk

½ cup granulated sugar

2 tsp. vanilla extract

½ tsp. ground cinnamon

½ tsp. ground nutmeg

½ tsp. salt

1 cup ripe but still firm bananas, sliced ¼ inch thick

Sauce

3 T. butter

2 T. granulated sugar

1 T. cornstarch

¾ cup milk

¼ cup light corn syrup

1 tsp. vanilla extract

Preheat the oven to 375°.

Place the bread cubes in a greased or buttered 2-quart casserole dish; pour the butter over the bread and toss to coat.

In a medium mixing bowl, lightly beat the eggs. Add the milk and then stir in the sugar, vanilla, cinnamon, nutmeg, and salt. Fold in the bananas. Pour over the bread cubes and mix well.

Bake uncovered for 40 to 50 minutes or until a knife inserted in the middle comes out clean.

While the pudding is baking, make the sauce. Melt the butter in a medium saucepan. Combine the sugar and cornstarch and add them to the butter. Stir in the milk and corn syrup. Cook, stirring constantly, until the mixture comes to a full boil. Boil for 1 minute, stirring constantly. Remove from the heat and stir in the vanilla.

Serve the warm sauce over the warm bread pudding.

Banana Nut Muffins

1½ cups unbleached all-purpose flour

1 tsp. baking soda

½ tsp. salt

½ tsp. ground cinnamon

½ cup (1 stick) butter, softened

¼ cup granulated sugar

3 very ripe bananas

2 eggs

1 tsp. vanilla extract

1 cup starter (active or discard)

¾ cup walnuts, chopped

Grease a 12-cup muffin tin or use paper cups that have been slightly sprayed with oil.

In a small mixing bowl, whisk together the flour, baking soda, salt, and cinnamon; set aside for now.

In a large mixing bowl, cream together the butter and sugar (use a hand mixer) until the mixture is well combined and smooth. Add the bananas and beat with the hand mixer until the bananas are thoroughly mashed and well combined. Add the eggs and vanilla and beat again until mixed completely. Add the starter and either mix on low just until combined or gently stir by hand. Fold in the walnuts. Evenly divide the batter into the prepared muffin tin.

Preheat the oven to 350° while the muffins rest for 15 minutes. Bake for 25 to 30 minutes or until a toothpick inserted into the middle comes out clean.

Cool the muffins in the tin for 10 minutes and then loosen the muffins by running a knife around the edges and place them on a wire rack to continue cooling. If you used paper liners, leave the muffins inside them and place them on a wire rack to cool.

Makes 12 muffins

Blackberry Hand Pies

1 double pie crust (see page167 for Pie Crust recipe), refrigerated until ready to use

4 cups fresh blackberries, boysenberries, or marionberries, washed

1 cup granulated sugar

¼ cup water

2 T. cornstarch mixed with 3 T. water

1 egg, beaten with 2 T. water for egg wash

1 cup powdered sugar

2 T. heavy cream

1 T. vanilla extract

In a medium saucepan, add the blackberries, sugar, and water. Heat on medium, stirring almost constantly, until the mixture comes to a boil. Add the cornstarch and water mixture to the blackberry mixture and stir constantly until the mixture thickens. Remove from the heat and let it cool and continue to thicken. (You can put the saucepan in the refrigerator or freezer to speed up the cooling process, but it will still need an hour or more to sufficiently cool down.)

Preheat the oven to 400°.

Divide the pie crust dough in half so it's easier to work with. Roll each portion of dough into a square or rectangle shape. Cut each portion of dough into 6 to 8 squares. Place about 2 tablespoons of the blackberry mixture slightly off-center on each square of dough. Brush the egg wash around the outer edges of the dough and then fold the dough over on itself to enclose the fruit filling. Use a fork to crimp the edges closed. Make a small slash on the top of each hand pie to vent the steam. Set the pies on a baking sheet that has been lined with a silicone baking mat or parchment paper.

continued...

Bake the pies in the preheated oven for 20 minutes or until done.

While the pies are baking, make the glaze. In a small bowl, whisk together the powdered sugar, heavy cream, and vanilla extract. Leave the mixture at room temperature until ready to use.

Allow the hand pies to cool a bit before glazing. They should be warm but not hot. Drizzle the glaze across the tops of the hand pies and let them continue to cool so the fruit filling thickens and the glaze hardens.

Makes 10 to 12 pies

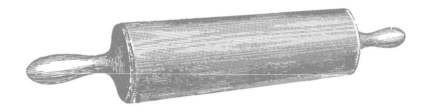

Blackberry Sourdough Bread Cobbler

4 cups blackberries

3 T. cornstarch

⅔ cup brown sugar

¼ cup granulated sugar

½ cup butter, melted and cooled slightly

1 egg, beaten

2 T. flour

½ tsp. ground cinnamon

4 cups cubed sourdough bread, about 1-inch squares

Preheat the oven to 350°. Butter or grease a 9 x 9-inch baking dish.

In a large bowl, mix the blackberries and cornstarch. Spread the fruit mixture evenly on the bottom of the prepared baking dish.

In a small bowl, mix the sugars, butter, egg, flour, and cinnamon until well combined and smooth.

Place the bread cubes on top of the blackberry mixture, pressing down gently and trying for an even top. Drizzle the sugar and butter mixture evenly over the top of the bread cubes.

Bake the cobbler for 35 to 45 minutes or until done. Let it cool for 10 minutes before serving. Extra good with vanilla ice cream or sweetened whipped cream.

Serves 4 to 6

Brownies

½ cup (1 stick) butter

12 oz. semisweet chocolate chips

½ cup cocoa powder

2 tsp. vanilla extract

2 eggs plus 1 egg yolk

1 cup granulated sugar

½ cup brown sugar

½ cup starter (discard)

1 cup unbleached all-purpose flour

1 tsp. salt

Preheat the oven to 350°. Line a 9 x 9-inch baking dish with parchment paper; set aside for now.

In a small saucepan, melt the butter on relatively low heat. Add the chocolate chips, cocoa powder, and vanilla extract, stirring constantly until the chocolate melts and the mixture is smooth. Remove from the heat and set it aside to cool to no more than 100°.

In a large mixing bowl, use an electric mixer to beat together the eggs, yolk, and sugars. Mix on low to medium speed for 3 minutes. Add the starter and melted chocolate mixture and beat on low speed until well combined. With a spatula, add the flour and salt and mix by hand just until combined. The batter will be heavy and thick.

Spoon the batter into the prepared baking dish and smooth the top. Bake for 35 to 40 minutes or until done in the middle. Allow the brownies to cool in the pan before lifting them out, using the parchment paper to do so, and then cut them into squares.

Serve them plain, with a scoop of ice cream, or sprinkled with powdered sugar.

Makes 9 (3-inch) or 12 (2-inch) brownies

Challah

Starter

226 g. bread flour or unbleached all-purpose flour

113 g. active starter

113 g. water

Bread dough

60 g. water

60 g. granulated sugar

55 g. vegetable oil

3 eggs, plus 1 more for brushing the braid

8 g. salt

400 g. bread flour or unbleached all-purpose flour

2 tsp. sesame seeds or poppy seeds or a combination of both (optional)

The night before:

In a medium bowl, mix all starter ingredients.

The starter will be thick and stiff, but work at it until all ingredients are incorporated; you can let the mixture sit for about a half hour and then mix again to thoroughly combine if necessary. Cover the bowl and let it sit at room temperature overnight.

The next morning:

In a large mixing bowl, combine the water, sugar, oil, 3 eggs, and salt; whisk until well combined and the sugar and salt are dissolved. Mix in the flour using a wooden spoon or your hands. At this point, the dough will be shaggy, stiff, and dry.

Flour your work surface and turn out the dough. Add the prepared starter (I try to make a large divot in the middle of the dough to corral it) and knead the dough until it is smooth and satiny (about 10 minutes); add a bit more flour to help with sticking, or add a tablespoon or two of water if the dough is so stiff that it's hard to knead. Place the worked dough in a greased or oiled large mixing bowl; cover with plastic wrap and let it sit at room temperature for 2 hours.

Line a baking sheet with parchment paper and set aside for now.

Divide the dough into 4 equal portions. (If you prefer a 3-braid challah, divide the dough into 3 equal portions.) Cover the dough pieces with a towel and let them rest for 15 minutes.

continued...

Roll each portion into a long, thin log about the length of the baking sheet. If the dough keeps wanting to shrink back, cover the dough again and let it continue to rest for another 15 minutes.

Place the log strands side by side on the baking sheet and pinch the 4 top ends together. To braid, grab the log on the far right; pass it over the next strand, under the third strand, and then over the fourth; the log strand that started out on the far right is now on the far-left side. Repeat this braiding, always starting from the far-right side, until the entire loaf has been braided. Pinch the ends at the bottom and then tuck both ends underneath the loaf to hide the pinches.

Cover the braided loaf with plastic wrap (don't cover it tightly, though) and let the dough rise until well bulked up—at least doubled or even tripled in size (5 to 7 hours).

Preheat the oven to 350°.

While the oven is preheating, beat the last egg in a small bowl until very well mixed. Brush the top of the braid with the beaten egg and then sprinkle the seeds on the top if using. Bake the challah for 35 to 40 minutes in the upper third of the oven. If the bread seems to be browning too quickly, place a tent of aluminum foil over the top to finish baking.

Set the challah bread on a wire rack until it is completely cool.

Makes 1 braid

Chocolate Cake

2 cups unbleached all-purpose flour

1¼ cups granulated sugar

¾ cup cocoa powder

1 tsp. baking powder

½ tsp. baking soda

½ tsp. salt

2 eggs

¾ cup sourdough discard

¾ cup oil

¼ cup sour cream

1 tsp. vanilla extract

1 cup boiling water

Preheat the oven to 350°. Grease a 9 x 13-inch baking dish or 2 round cake pans.

In a large mixing bowl, whisk together the flour, sugar, cocoa powder, baking powder, baking soda, and salt. Add the eggs, starter, oil, sour cream, and vanilla and stir to mix well; the batter will be extremely thick at this point. Pour in the boiling water and stir until the batter is fully mixed and smooth.

Pour the batter into the prepared pan(s) and bake for 35 to 45 minutes or until a toothpick inserted into the middle comes out clean. Set the pan on a wire rack and cover the cake with a clean kitchen towel to cool before frosting if desired.

Chocolate Chip Muffins

1¼ cups unbleached all-purpose flour

¾ cup granulated sugar

2 tsp. baking powder

½ tsp. salt

1 egg

½ cup starter

⅓ cup oil or melted butter

3 T. milk

1 cup chocolate chips

Coarse sugar for sprinkling

Preheat the oven to 400°. Line a muffin tin with paper liners.

In a large mixing bowl, whisk together the flour, sugar, baking powder, and salt.

In a separate bowl, whisk together the egg, starter, oil or melted butter, and milk. Pour the wet mixture into the flour mixture and stir just until mixed; the batter will be somewhat lumpy. Add the chocolate chips and gently fold into the batter. Fill the muffin cups evenly about two-thirds full. Sprinkle coarse sugar on top of each muffin.

Bake for 18 to 23 minutes or until a toothpick inserted into the middle of a muffin comes out clean or with a few moist crumbs attached. Remove the muffins from the tin and cool them on a wire rack.

Makes 12 muffins

Coffee Cake

Topping

¼ cup granulated sugar

¼ cup unbleached all-purpose flour

2 T. butter, melted

½ tsp. ground cinnamon

Cake

1 cup active starter

⅓ cup vegetable oil

1 egg, beaten

½ tsp. vanilla extract

1 cup unbleached all-purpose flour

1 cup granulated sugar

1 tsp. baking soda

1 tsp. ground cinnamon

½ tsp. salt

Place the topping ingredients in a small bowl and use a fork to roughly mix together just until you achieve coarse crumbs.

Preheat the oven to 350°. Grease a 9 x 9-inch baking dish and set aside for now.

In a medium mixing bowl, blend together the starter, oil, egg, and vanilla.

In a separate bowl, whisk together the flour, sugar, baking soda, cinnamon, and salt. Add the flour mixture to the starter mixture and stir to blend.

Spoon the batter into the prepared baking dish (it will be very thick) and then sprinkle the crumb mixture over the top.

Bake in the preheated oven for 40 to 45 minutes or until done. Cool in the pan for about 10 minutes before serving.

9 servings

Corn Fritters

1 cup flour

½ cup nonfat dry milk

½ tsp. baking soda

½ tsp. salt

2 eggs

1 cup starter (fresh is better, but you can use discard at room temperature)

1 cup corn, fresh, canned and drained, or frozen and thawed

1 tsp. finely minced onion

Vegetable oil for frying

In a medium mixing bowl, whisk together the flour, dry milk, baking soda, and salt. Set it aside for now.

In a large mixing bowl, beat eggs. Stir in the starter, corn, and onion. Add the flour mixture and stir just until combined.

Pour 2 to 3 inches of oil in a deep-sided cast-iron skillet (or other suitable, heavy-duty pan) and heat the oil to about 375°. Drop the dough into the hot oil, about a tablespoon per fritter, and fry for about 2 minutes; turn the fritters over and cook the second side for about 2 minutes. The fritters should be golden brown when done. Drain on paper towels and serve them hot.

Makes about 2 dozen, depending on size

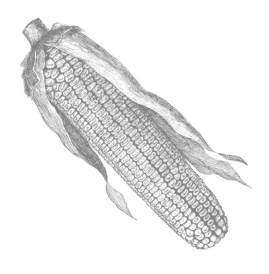

Crackers

2 T. butter

200 g. (¾ cup) starter discard, stirred down before weighing or measuring

¼ tsp. salt

¼ tsp. coarse salt for sprinkling

Preheat the oven to 325°. Cut a piece of parchment paper to fit inside a baking sheet or use a silicone baking mat if it fits.

In a microwave-safe medium bowl, melt the butter and allow to cool to about 100°. Add the starter and salt (not the coarse salt) and mix well.

Spread a thin layer of the mixture onto the parchment paper using a spatula, an off-set knife, or the back of a spoon. The thinner you can spread the mixture, the crisper the crackers will be once baked. Sprinkle the top of the dough with coarse salt.

Bake for 10 minutes and then remove the baking sheet and score the dough into crackers the size you want. (Use a pizza cutter or knife to score.) Return the baking sheet to the oven and continue to bake for an additional 20 to 30 minutes, checking once every 5 minutes after the first 20 minutes to make sure they don't burn.

Amounts vary, depending on size and thickness of crackers

Crepes

1 cup starter

3 eggs, beaten

2 T. butter, melted

¼ tsp. salt

¼ to ½ cup milk to thin batter

Oil or butter for frying, plus more butter for brushing the tops of the crepes

Heat a 10-inch crepe pan or skillet over medium heat.

In a medium mixing bowl (a bowl with a pour spout makes it easy to pour the batter into the pan when cooking), stir together the starter, eggs, melted butter, and salt. Stir well so no lumps remain, adding milk to get the consistency of heavy whipping cream.

Pour about ¼ cup of batter into the center of the prepared pan and then tilt the pan using a circular motion to distribute the batter evenly. Cook for about 1 minute or until the edges start to pull away from the pan and the top of the crepe looks a bit dry; use tongs or a spatula to flip the crepe and cook the second side for another minute or so. Place the crepe on a plate and brush the tops with butter so they don't stick together while you are cooking the remainder.

Crepes can be eaten plain or sprinkled with powdered sugar. But they are even better if you roll them up around savory or sweet ingredients. Here are a few ideas to get you started:

- Cooked bacon, scrambled eggs, and shredded cheese
- Chicken and mushrooms baked with béchamel sauce (sometimes I add spinach and ricotta or shredded Gruyère cheese)
- Smoked salmon, thinly sliced red onion, and cream cheese
- Peach slices sweetened with brown sugar and rolled up in the crepe, with sliced fresh strawberries and a dollop of sour cream on top (this is one of our favorites!)
- Fresh fruit (blueberries, raspberries, pitted cherries, etc.) with sweetened whipped cream
- Fried banana slices drizzled with melted chocolate or caramel syrup

Makes 6 crepes

Crumb Topping for Muffins

½ cup granulated sugar

½ cup unbleached all-purpose flour

3 T. butter, melted

Place the ingredients in a small bowl and use a fork to roughly mix together until you achieve a coarse crumb.

When ready to use, top your prepared muffins with the crumbs, gently pushing them into the batter so they stay on as the muffins bake.

Donuts with Various Toppings

2 cups unbleached all-purpose flour

½ cup sugar

1 tsp. baking powder

½ tsp. baking soda

½ tsp. salt

¼ tsp. ground cinnamon (optional)

1 egg

½ cup starter (discard or active)

⅓ cup buttermilk (you can substitute regular milk, but the donuts won't be as puffy)

2 T. oil

Oil for frying

Topping of your choice (see below)

In a medium mixing bowl, whisk together the flour, sugar, baking powder, baking soda, salt, and cinnamon if using. Set it aside for now.

In a large mixing bowl, stir together egg, starter, buttermilk, and 2 tablespoons of oil. Add the flour mixture and stir just until the dough comes together. Turn out the dough onto a floured work surface and gently knead the dough for 1 minute. Cover it with a kitchen towel and let it rest for 5 minutes to relax the dough.

Pour about 2 inches of oil into a cast-iron deep-sided skillet and heat the oil to 360°. Place paper towels on a large plate or baking sheet and set aside for now.

Roll out the dough to 2 inches thick and cut out the donuts. Reform the scraps of dough to make as many donuts as possible. (The last one or two donuts might be misshapen, but that's fine.) Fry the donuts until golden, about 2 minutes per side. Use a slotted spoon to turn the donuts and to remove them from the hot oil; place the fried donuts on the paper towels to drain.

Makes 8 to 10 donuts, depending on their size

Donut Toppings:

- Sprinkle with granulated sugar
- Sprinkle with cinnamon sugar
- Sprinkle with powdered sugar
- Frost with vanilla or chocolate frosting and sprinkle with cake decorations
- Make a glaze with powdered sugar and water or milk and drizzle it on the tops
- Make the donuts without the hole in the middle and use a food baster to insert pudding, jam, or jelly into the middle

Dumplings

1 cup starter

1 cup unbleached all-purpose flour

2 T. vegetable oil

1 egg

2 tsp. baking powder

¼ tsp. baking soda

½ tsp. salt

Note: This dumpling recipe is used with savory food. The dumplings are cooked in food such as stews or soups.

In a medium mixing bowl, combine all ingredients. Drop walnut-sized portions into the simmering food and give the contents a gentle stir so the dumplings stay separate while cooking. Cover the pot and cook the dumplings until cooked through—at least 15 minutes.

Makes about 20 dumplings, depending on size

Focaccia

(Refer to A Basic Sourdough Bread Loaf on page 26 for instructions and techniques.)

493 g. unbleached all-purpose flour (or use 345 g. unbleached all-purpose flour and 148 g. bread flour)

394 g. water, divided

94 g. lively starter

9 g. salt

10 g. olive oil, plus more for topping the focaccia

For toppings: coarse salt, fresh or dried herbs, minced garlic, halved cherry tomatoes, sliced black or green olives, Parmesan cheese, etc.

Early in the day, use a large mixing bowl to stir together the flour, 344 g. of the water, and the starter and salt. When the dough begins to form a ball, continue to mix and knead by hand for about 5 minutes. Slowly add the remaining 50 g. of water, a bit at a time, mixing and kneading each time you add more water, until the mixture forms into a soft, smooth dough. Add the olive oil, a bit at a time, mixing and kneading each time you add more oil, until the mixture forms into a soft, smooth dough.

Using a dough scraper or silicone spatula, scrape the dough into a large, clean mixing bowl. Cover the bowl with plastic wrap and let it rest at room temperature for about 30 minutes.

Stretch and fold the dough at half-hour intervals a total of 4 times, covering the bowl after each time.

Generously grease a 9 x 13-inch baking sheet (the kind that has low sides); use about 2 tablespoons of oil to grease the pan.

continued...

Gently transfer the dough to the greased pan and stretch the dough to the corners of the baking sheet; cover with plastic wrap and let it rest for 2 hours, uncovering the dough every 30 minutes and pulling the dough once again to the corners of the pan. During this time, the dough is relaxing and stretching and will begin to stay relaxed at the corners of the pan. With the dough covered, let it rest in the baking sheet for 2 hours.

Preheat the oven to 450°. While the oven is preheating, wet your knuckles and press a knuckle into the top of the focaccia about 2 inches apart, pressing all the way down to the bottom of the dough. Brush or drizzle 1 to 2 tablespoons of olive oil over the top and then sprinkle on desired toppings. Bake the focaccia for 30 to 40 minutes or until it's golden brown on top. Remove from the oven and cool for 5 minutes in the pan before removing the focaccia to a wire rack to cool further.

Fried Fish

2 cups starter

2 tsp. salt, or 2 tsp. Old Bay Seasoning

½ tsp. black pepper

½ tsp. paprika

1 tsp. baking powder

6 pieces boneless, skinless whitefish filets (such as cod, halibut, or tilapia), either left whole or chunked into pieces

Oil for frying (choose an oil with a high smoke point)

In a large mixing bowl, stir together the starter, salt or Old Bay Seasoning, pepper, and paprika.

Pour about 4 inches of oil in a deep-sided cast-iron skillet or pot and heat the oil to 375°.

Right before you are ready to fry the fish, add the baking powder to the starter mixture and stir. Coat the fish pieces and then drop them carefully into the hot oil. Fry the fish for 2 to 3 minutes or until the batter is golden and crisp; using tongs or a slotted spoon, turn the fish over and fry the second side about 2 more minutes or until done. Set the fried fish on paper towels to drain and eat them while they're hot.

We like these dipped in malt vinegar, but tartar sauce is good too.

Serves 6

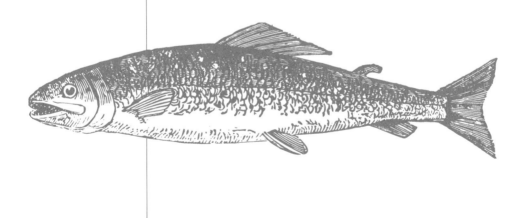

Fried Onion Rings

Peanut, avocado, or canola oil for frying

1 cup unbleached all-purpose flour

1 tsp. salt or seasoned salt

½ tsp. pepper (optional)

2 cups starter discard

3 onions (more or less), outer skin peeled and cut into ½-inch-thick rings

Note: This is a very flexible recipe. You can cut this recipe in half if you don't have enough starter discard, but keep in mind that you can use whatever amount of starter you have and simply fry onion rings until you're out of starter. The ratio for starter to flour is 2:1.

In a deep-sided skillet or large pot, slowly heat about 3 inches of oil on medium-low to 370°.

Preheat the oven to 200°. Place paper towels on a baking sheet and set aside for now. Line another baking sheet with parchment paper or lay the parchment paper on the kitchen counter.

In a low-sided bowl or plate, mix the flour, salt, and pepper.

Stir the starter discard and then pour it into a bowl.

Separate the layers of the onions; dip them one ring at a time into the starter and then coat them with the flour mixture; set the prepared onion rings onto the parchment paper.

Fry the onion rings in batches so they don't crowd the pot. Turn the onion rings over if necessary to fry both sides until they are golden brown and crisp. Remove the onion rings with a slotted spoon and place them on the baking sheet lined with paper towels. Put the baking sheet into the warm oven and continue frying in batches until done, making sure the temperature of the oil is 370° each time you add a new batch.

These are best eaten immediately.

Gingerbread

½ cup (1 stick) butter, softened to room temperature

¾ cup brown sugar

¼ cup granulated sugar

¾ cup molasses

2 eggs

1 cup starter (discard is fine)

½ tsp. baking soda

1 cup unbleached all-purpose flour

2 tsp. ground cinnamon

1½ tsp. ground ginger

½ tsp. ground cloves

½ tsp. salt

¼ cup heavy cream

¼ cup hot water

Preheat the oven to 350°. Line a 9 x 9-inch baking dish or 2 loaf pans with parchment paper sprayed with oil.

In a large mixing bowl and using an electric mixer, beat together the sugars and butter until smooth. Beat in the molasses and then add the eggs one at a time, beating after each addition. Add the starter and baking soda and beat on low speed just until combined.

In a separate bowl, whisk together the flour, cinnamon, ginger, cloves, and salt. Add to the wet ingredients and beat on low speed just until combined. Beat in the cream and then the hot water. Place the batter into the prepared baking dish or evenly divide between the 2 loaf pans.

If using a baking dish, bake for 40 to 50 minutes or until a toothpick inserted into the middle comes out clean. If using 2 loaf pans, bake about 10 minutes more and test for doneness by inserting a toothpick into the middle of one of the loaves.

Cool in the pan(s) for 15 minutes and then gently remove the gingerbread using the parchment paper and place on a wire rack to cool further.

Serve plain or with a dollop of sweetened whipped cream or scoop of vanilla ice cream on top.

Makes 9 to 12 servings

Glazed Donuts

Donuts

¼ cup milk

¼ cup granulated sugar

¼ cup (½ stick) butter, cut into 4 pieces

2 eggs

2⅓ to 2⅔ cups unbleached all-purpose flour, divided

⅔ cup active starter

1 tsp. salt

Glaze

¼ cup butter

2 tsp. vanilla extract

2 cups powdered sugar

2 to 3 T. milk

In a small saucepan, heat the milk, granulated sugar, and butter, stirring to melt the butter and dissolve the sugar. Take off the heat and let the mixture cool until barely warm—just above room temperature.

In a stand mixer, pour in the milk mixture and then add the eggs, 2 cups of the flour, and the starter and salt. Turn to low speed and mix until a wet dough forms. Turn the mixer to medium-low speed and knead the dough for 4 to 5 minutes. Let the dough rest in the mixer bowl for 10 minutes. Add another ⅓ cup flour, turn the mixer to low until the flour has been incorporated into the dough, and then turn to medium-low speed and knead the dough for another 4 to 5 minutes.

Turn out the dough onto a floured work surface and knead by hand, using as little extra flour as possible, until the dough is no longer sticky but is still soft and tender. Shape the dough into a ball.

Lightly grease a large mixing bowl and place the dough ball inside. Cover the dough with plastic wrap or a damp kitchen towel and let the dough rise at room temperature for 3 to 4 hours.

Carefully turn out the dough onto a lightly floured work surface and roll the dough to about ¾ inch thick. Use as little flour as possible to keep the dough from sticking. Cut out the donuts and place them on greased baking sheets 1-inch apart. Reroll the trimmed dough to make as many donuts as possible. Cover the baking sheets with damp kitchen towels and let them rest at room temperature for about 2 hours. They should be slightly risen when ready to fry.

Fill a cast-iron deep-sided skillet with about 3 inches of oil and heat the oil to 370 to 375°.

While the oil is heating, make the glaze: In a microwave-safe bowl, melt the butter. Add the vanilla and stir to mix. Next, add the powdered sugar and stir, adding the milk a tablespoon at a time until a slightly thick glaze is made. (When you dip the fried donuts into the glaze, it will melt and coat the donuts.)

Fry the donuts for 1 to 2 minutes per side and the donut holes about 30 seconds per side, being careful not to crowd them in the skillet. Use a slotted spoon to remove the donuts from the hot oil and place them on baking sheets lined with paper towels to drain.

When the donuts are cool enough to be picked up, dip the hot donuts into the glaze. You can stop at one side, or dip both sides to complete-ly cover each donut.

Makes 12 to 14 donuts and at least a dozen donut holes if desired, depending on size

Lemon Blueberry Muffins

1¼ cups unbleached all-purpose flour

½ cup granulated sugar

2 tsp. baking powder

½ tsp. salt

1 egg

⅓ cup milk

⅓ cup oil

¼ cup starter (discard)

½ tsp. food-grade lemon oil or 1 tsp. lemon extract

1 cup blueberries

2 tsp. coarse sugar for sprinkling

Preheat the oven to 375°. Line a muffin tin with paper liners or spray with oil; set aside for now.

In a large mixing bowl, whisk together the flour, sugar, baking powder, and salt. Add the egg, milk, oil, starter, and lemon oil. Mix until the ingredients are combined, but try not to overmix. Fold in the blueberries and spoon the batter into the prepared muffin cups. Sprinkle coarse sugar on the top of each muffin or top with Crumb Topping (recipe on page 152).

Bake for 25 to 28 minutes or until golden on top and a toothpick inserted into the middle comes out clean. Cool on a wire rack.

Makes 6 large or about 9 regular muffins

Molasses Cookies

2 cups unbleached all-purpose flour

2 tsp. baking powder

1 tsp. ground cinnamon

1 tsp. ground ginger

¼ tsp. nutmeg

¼ tsp. ground cloves

¼ tsp. salt

1 cup brown sugar

½ cup starter, active or discard (active will make puffier cookies while discard will make the cookies chewier)

¼ cup shortening

¼ cup molasses

1 egg

Granulated sugar to roll the cookies in before baking

Preheat the oven to 350°. Prepare a baking sheet by greasing it or layering a silicone baking mat or parchment paper on the sheet.

In a medium mixing bowl, whisk together the flour, baking powder, cinnamon, ginger, nutmeg, cloves, and salt; set aside for now.

In a large mixing bowl, stir together the brown sugar, starter, shortening, molasses, and egg using an electric hand mixer or by hand. Mix until the ingredients are smooth. Add the flour mixture and stir until fully combined.

Roll the dough into 1-inch balls and then roll each ball in granulated sugar. Place the balls of dough onto the prepared baking sheet and bake for 9 to 11 minutes or until done. (You'll need to bake in two or three batches.)

Remove the cookies from the baking sheet and set them on a wire rack to cool.

Makes 2 dozen

Noodles

1½ cups unbleached all-purpose flour

½ cup starter (discard or active)

2 eggs

2 T. salt

Place all ingredients into a stand mixer that has a dough hook attachment. Mix on low speed until the dough forms a ball. Remove the dough from the mixer and wrap it in plastic wrap. (You will probably need some flour to keep the dough from sticking to your hands and the plastic wrap.) Let the dough rest at room temperature for 30 minutes.

Take portions of the dough and place them on a floured work surface. Using a floured rolling pin, roll the pieces out to as thin as you desire. Using a sharp knife or a pizza cutter, slice the dough into noodles to your desired length and width. Let the noodles sit at room temperature while you prepare the cooking pot.

Fill a large pot with water and the salt; place on the stove and heat the contents to a rolling boil. Drop the noodles into the boiling water and cook, stirring occasionally to keep them from sticking together, for 3 to 5 minutes or until tender and done. (The cook time could be longer if your noodles are extra thick.) Drain and serve.

Makes 4 to 6 servings

Oatmeal Cookies

1 cup starter, active or discard

1 cup shortening or butter

2 eggs

1 tsp. vanilla extract

2 cups unbleached all-purpose or whole wheat flour

1 cup rolled oats

1 cup granulated sugar

½ cup brown sugar

1 tsp. salt

1 tsp. baking soda

1 tsp. baking powder

¼ tsp. ground cardamom (optional, but it really enhances the flavor)

Up to 1 cup of chocolate chips, raisins, and/or chopped nuts (optional)

Preheat the oven to 375°. Line a baking sheet with a silicone baking mat or parchment paper.

In a large mixing bowl and using an electric mixer, cream together the starter and shortening. Add the eggs one at a time, beating after each until thoroughly mixed together; add the vanilla and mix again.

In another mixing bowl, stir together the flour, oats, sugars, salt, baking soda, baking powder, and cardamom if using. Add the flour mixture to the starter mixture a bit at a time and stir by hand to combine. Add the chocolate chips, raisins, or chopped nuts if using and stir well again to mix thoroughly.

Drop by the tablespoonful onto the prepared baking sheet and bake for 10 minutes or until done. Place on wire racks to cool. (This recipe makes a lot of cookies, and because I don't have enough wire cooling racks, I place brown paper or wax paper on the kitchen counter and place the cookies there to cool.)

Makes about 5 dozen

Peach Cobbler

3 lbs. ripe peaches

½ cup granulated sugar plus 4 T., divided

1 T. lemon juice

½ tsp ground cinnamon

½ tsp. vanilla extract

1 T. cornstarch

½ heaping cup unbleached all-purpose flour

½ tsp. baking powder

½ tsp. baking soda

¼ tsp. salt

5 T. very cold butter, cut into small pieces the size of walnuts

1 cup starter discard

Preheat the oven to 375°. Butter or grease a 9 x 9-inch baking dish; set aside for now.

Wash the peaches and slice thinly; no need to peel unless you prefer them that way. Place the sliced peaches into a large mixing bowl and add ½ cup sugar, lemon juice, cinnamon, and vanilla extract. Gently mix until well combined. Taste the mixture and add more sugar if needed. Sprinkle the cornstarch over the peach mixture and mix well. Place the peaches into the prepared baking dish and set aside for now.

In a separate mixing bowl, whisk together the flour, 2 tablespoons of sugar, baking powder, baking soda, and salt. Add the butter to the flour mixture using a pastry cutter or two forks to cut the butter into the flour mixture until it resembles coarse crumbles. Add the starter and mix until the dough forms; it will barely hold together at this point. With your hands, gently mix and knead the dough until it comes together, adding more flour if needed.

Grab pieces of the dough and pat them into thin "biscuits" ½ to ¾ inch thick. Lay the "biscuits" on top of the peach mixture, leaving a bit of room around the outside so steam can escape when baking. Sprinkle the top of the cobbler with the remaining 2 tablespoons of sugar.

Bake for 35 to 40 minutes or until the top is golden brown around the edges of the crust. Remove from the oven and allow to cool for about 10 minutes before serving.

Serves 4 to 6

Pie Crust

113 g. very cold butter (1 stick)

125 g. unbleached all-purpose flour

3 g. salt

2 g. granulated sugar

125 g. discard starter (discard straight from the refrigerator works best)

5 g. white vinegar

Note: While this pie crust can be used interchangeably with regular pie crust, I think it's especially delicious when used for making savory dishes.

Shred the butter with a cheese grater into a large mixing bowl. Work quickly so the butter remains as cold as possible.

In another bowl, whisk together the flour, salt, and sugar; add these ingredients to the mixing bowl and toss the ingredients to coat and separate the butter shreds. Continue with a pastry cutter to cut the butter into the flour mixture until it forms large crumbs.

Add the discard starter and vinegar and use a fork to combine them with the flour mixture. When the dough begins to hold together, switch to your hands and quickly work the dough so there are no more dry bits of flour. If the dough seems too dry, you can add a teaspoon or two of very cold water (ice water if you have it).

Shape the dough into a flattened disc; wrap in plastic wrap and roll through the plastic to further flatten and smooth the edges of the dough. Refrigerate the dough at least 2 hours.

When ready to use the crust, remove the dough from the plastic wrap and place the dough on a floured work surface. Flour a rolling pin and the top of the dough and roll out the pie crust. When you lay the crust into the pie plate, use your fingers to gently press it into place.

Bake according to your regular pie crust directions.

Makes 1 single crust. Double the ingredients to make a top and bottom crust.

Rosemary Wheat Crackers

1 cup starter discard

½ cup whole wheat flour

½ cup unbleached all-purpose flour

¼ cup butter, softened

2 T. dried rosemary, or ¼ cup fresh snipped rosemary

½ tsp. salt

Olive or vegetable oil for brushing

¼ to ½ tsp. coarse salt for sprinkling

In a large mixing bowl, mix the starter, flours, butter, rosemary, and salt. Begin mixing with a large spoon or spatula and then change to using your hands to finish; the dough should be smooth and thoroughly mixed.

Divide the dough into 2 pieces; form each portion into a flattened ball and wrap each portion tightly in plastic wrap. Refrigerate for 1 hour.

Preheat the oven to 350°.

Cut a piece of parchment paper to the size of the baking sheet you plan to use or use a silicone baking mat. Lightly flour the liner.

Remove one of the portions of dough and lay it on the floured liner. Lightly flour a rolling pin and roll out the dough as thin as possible.

Using a light touch, brush the tops of the crackers with the oil and then sprinkle the coarse salt over the top. Score the dough to make square or rectangle shapes and then poke a fork 2 times on the surface of each cracker. Transfer the liner onto the baking sheet and bake for 20 to 25 minutes or until golden brown. Transfer the crackers along with the liner they baked on to a cooling rack to cool completely before breaking apart.

Repeat these steps for the second portion of dough.

Amounts vary, depending on size of crackers

Tortillas

¾ cup water

½ cup starter (discard is fine)

3 cups unbleached all-purpose flour

1¼ tsp. salt

1 tsp. baking powder

2 T. vegetable shortening

In a small mixing bowl, stir together the water and starter; set aside for now.

In a larger mixing bowl, whisk together the flour, salt, and baking powder. Add the shortening and, with a fork or your hands, mix together until well combined. You don't want any large pieces of shortening.

Pour in the starter mixture and combine with your hands until everything is completely mixed together and there are no bits of dry flour. Shape the dough into a ball and let it rest in the bowl, covered (I like to use plastic wrap) and on the counter, for about 30 minutes.

Cut the dough ball into 16 equal pieces; roll each piece into a small ball and lay them on parchment paper or a silicone baking mat and cover to rest for another 30 minutes.

When ready to cook them, roll each ball into a thin circle about 6 inches in diameter (use flour to keep them from sticking if need be). Cook on a preheated skillet or cast-iron tortilla pan, using a bit of shortening or oil if needed to prevent sticking to the pan. Cook until bubbles form and the underside has browned; flip the tortilla and cook the second side until done.

Use them as you would regular tortillas, but they are also delicious fresh from the skillet with butter spread over the top. If you don't use them all in one sitting, you can refrigerate the leftover tortillas and simply heat them on the skillet when ready to use.

Makes 16 tortillas

Vanilla Cake

1½ cups unbleached all-purpose flour

1½ tsp. baking powder

¼ tsp. salt

6 T. butter, softened to room temperature

¾ cup granulated sugar

2 eggs

½ cup milk

½ cup starter

1½ tsp. vanilla extract

Preheat the oven to 350°. Line an 8 x 8-inch baking dish with parchment paper that has been sprayed with cooking oil or grease the baking dish and then dust with flour. Set aside for now.

In a medium mixing bowl, whisk together the flour, baking powder, and salt and mix well. Add the butter to the flour mixture and use an electric mixer to cream together the flour mixture and butter; beat until smooth (about 2 minutes). Add the sugar and beat the mixture until light and fluffy (about 3 minutes). Add the eggs, one at a time, and beat well after each addition. Next, add the milk, starter, and vanilla and gently but thoroughly beat until the mixture is fully combined and smooth.

Pour the batter into the prepared baking dish and bake in the preheated oven for 30 minutes or until the cake is done; a toothpick inserted into the middle of the cake should come out clean.

Cool the cake before frosting if desired, but it's good eaten plain as well.

Serves 9

Vanilla Muffins

1½ cups unbleached all-purpose flour

⅔ cup granulated sugar

1 T. baking powder

¼ tsp. salt

1 egg

½ cup starter discard

½ cup oil or melted butter

⅓ cup milk

1 tsp. vanilla extract

Preheat the oven to 425°. Line a muffin tin with paper liners or spray with oil; set aside for now.

In a large mixing bowl, whisk together the flour, sugar, baking powder, and salt.

In a separate bowl, whisk together the egg, starter, oil or melted butter, milk, and vanilla until well mixed.

Pour the egg mixture into the flour mixture and stir just until combined; do not overmix. Divide the batter evenly among the prepared muffin cups.

Turn down the oven to 350° and immediately place the muffins in the oven to bake. Bake for 15 to 18 minutes or until a toothpick inserted in the middle comes out with moist crumbs but not too wet.

Makes 10 muffins

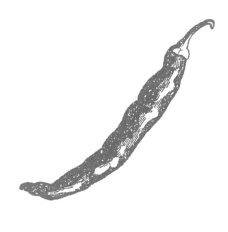

Wheat Muffins

Starter

240 g. unbleached all-purpose flour

240 g. water

1 to 2 T. stored starter

Muffins

Active starter from above

1 egg, beaten

120 g. milk

140 g. unbleached, all-purpose flour

140 g. whole wheat flour

2 T. granulated sugar

1 tsp. salt

¼ cup butter

Prepare the active starter the night before. (If you plan to bake in the evening, prepare the starter early in the day so it can activate.)

The night before:

In a large mixing bowl, combine all starter ingredients and mix well to thoroughly combine. Cover the bowl with plastic wrap and let it sit at room temperature until the starter has about doubled in bulk and is bubbly and frothy.

The next day:

In the large mixing bowl that contains the active starter, add the egg and milk; mix to thoroughly combine.

In another bowl, whisk together the flours, sugar, and salt. With a pastry cutter or fork, cut the butter into the flour mixture, working until the mixture is in small crumbles. Add this mixture into the large bowl with the starter mixture and stir until the batter is moist but not entirely lump-free; do not overmix.

Line a muffin tin with paper or silicone liners and spoon the batter into the cups about two-thirds full. Let the muffins sit at room temperature for 1 hour. While the muffins are resting, preheat the oven to 400°. Bake the muffins for 20 to 25 minutes or until done. Remove the muffins from the tin and allow them to cool on a wire rack.

Makes about 12 muffins

RESOURCES

Amazon.com Amazon sells starters as well as lots of tools for your sourdough baking needs, such as cast-iron Dutch ovens and bread bakers, bannetons/proofing baskets, proofing boxes, loaf pans, linen cloth, lames, and storage containers.

Breadtopia.com Besides sourdough starters for sale, Breadtopia offers a wide array of baking tools and kitchen gadgets, many of them geared toward sourdough.

Carlsfriends.net For years, Carl Griffith gave away batches of his family's sourdough starter to anyone who asked. Dubbed the 1847 Oregon Trail Sourdough Starter, the mother starter had been in the Griffith family for 150 years when Carl passed away in 2000. Since then, a few of Carl's friends have kept their starters going and sent some to anyone who wanted their own.

Culturesforhealth.com The Cultures for Health website has a lot going on, including wonderful choices for your sourdough needs. I have bought many things over the years from this company and have never been disappointed.

KingArthurBaking.com King Arthur pretty much has everything you could possibly dream of needing. Their flour is good quality, and they have recipes that will inspire.

Sourdo.com This website offers 17 different sourdough cultures from around the world—Bahrain, Egypt, Finland, Russia, the Yukon, and more.

Yemoos.com Yemoos offers sourdough cultures as well as other nourishing cultures and kits. One of the reasons I like this website is that it's run by a family.

RECIPE INDEX

BLESS YOUR FAMILY WITH HEALTHY, ORGANIC FOOD

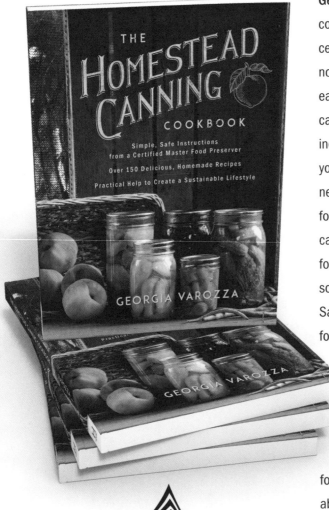

Georgia Varozza is not only a cooking enthusiast but also a certified master food preserver, and now she shows you how safe and easy canning your favorite foods can be. She teaches you the basics, including how to fit the process into your busy life, the equipment you'll need, and step-by-step instructions for both water-bath and pressure canning. Enjoy wholesome recipes for canning fruit, vegetables, meat, soups, sauces, and so much more. Save money by preserving your own food and gain valuable peace of mind by knowing **exactly** what's going into the meals you're serving. Join the growing number of households who are embracing the pioneer lifestyle. It's time for you and your family to feel good about food again. This cookbook can help.

TEN PEAKS PRESS™
EUGENE, OR